Taking French Feminism to the Streets

Fadela Amara and the Rise of *Ni Putes Ni Soumises*

Edited and Translated by
Brittany Murray and Diane Perpich

University of Illinois Press
URBANA, CHICAGO, AND SPRINGFIELD

Portions of this work were originally
published as *La racaille de la République*
by Fadela Amara and Mohammed Abdi,

Manufactured in the United States of America
C 5 4 3 2 1
∞ This book is printed on acid-free paper.

Library of Congress Cataloging-in-Publication Data
Taking French feminism to the streets : Fadela Amara and the rise of
Ni Putes Ni Soumises / edited and translated by Brittany Murray and
Diane Perpich.
p. cm.
"Portions of this work were originally published as *La racaille de la République* by Fadela Amara and Mohammed Abdi, Editions du Seuil, 2006"—T.p. verso.
Includes index.
ISBN 978-0-252-03548-7 (hbk. : alk. paper)
1. Amara, Fadela. 2. Ni putes ni soumises (Organization).
3. Feminism—France. 4. Sex discrimination against women—France.
5. Muslim women—France—Social conditions.
6. Women—France—Social conditions. 7. Immigrants—France—
Social conditions. I. Murray, Brittany. II. Perpich, Diane. III. Amara,
Fadela. Racaille de la République.
HQ1613.T35 2011
305.48'6970944—dc23 2011027793

Contents

Taking French Feminism to the Streets

Introduction. Mapping the Terrain

Ni Putes Ni Soumises in Context

Brittany Murray and Diane Perpich

A Special Assembly convening more than two hundred women from France's most disenfranchised populations; a five-week-long march that stopped in public housing projects in twenty-three major French cities to address the conditions faced by women in France's most impoverished neighborhoods; a petition signed by more than eighty thousand people and delivered to the prime minister on the International Day of Women: Ni Putes Ni Soumises burst onto the French national stage in the spring of 2003 and rapidly became a media sensation. The name of the movement, Neither Whores Nor Submissive, was intentionally designed to shock people out of their complacency. Directed in equal measure against the strict control of women's bodies and sexuality in France's immigrant communities and against the media portrayal of Muslim and Arab women as submissive, docile, and complicit in their own oppression, the name and the movement rejected the relegation of women to anything less than their full place in society. In many respects, the women and men who joined forces under the banner of Ni Putes Ni Soumises were not asking for anything radically new. They were simply demanding respect and equality for all women in all aspects of life and in all of the Republic's neighborhoods. This was in many ways the feminism of Simone de Beauvoir, but now in the mouths of young women and men who were the children of parents from France's former colonies and protectorates, who were of Maghrebi, Arab, and North African descent, and who had grown up in some of France's most blighted neighborhoods.

Speaking out on the hot-button issues facing women in these neighborhoods, Ni Putes Ni Soumises (NPNS) denounced discriminatory practices in employment and housing, rejected the xenophobia of national immigration policies, decried the sexism of everyday life in the *quartiers*, and demanded a stop to all forms of violence against women. Such positions, coming from a multiethnic group representing politically and economically marginalized populations, were not unexpected. More surprising, and perhaps harder for North American and Anglophone feminists to digest, has been the movement's near-categorical rejection of the discourse of difference and all forms of identity politics in favor of the language of equal rights and universally shared political values. Shouldn't an advocate group for France's ethnically diverse neighborhoods be promoting multiculturalism and attention to difference? Wouldn't the particularity of these women's experience demand a rejection, or at least a revision, of France's historical preoccupation with assimilation and social cohesion?

Few academics anticipating the next wave of French feminist thought would have imagined a woman such as Fadela Amara, one of NPNS's founders, the movement's most recognizable spokeswoman, and its president from 2003 to 2007. Amara is the daughter of Algerian immigrants from the Maghreb, but she insists on her own French identity and emphasizes her love of her native country. She is a practicing Muslim and yet vehemently supports the ban on religious symbols, including the headscarf, in French public schools. Amara was raised in a housing project outside Clermont-Ferrand, an industrial area in the center of France. She has witnessed the effects of poverty, systematic racism, and police brutality firsthand, but she rejects the language of victimization and affirmative action (termed *discrimination positive* in French) in favor of laws and programs that promote personal responsibility and equality of opportunity across the board. In general, Amara and the NPNS movement reject policies that single out ethnic, cultural, or religious groups for special treatment, whether for ill or for good. Likewise, they insist on the importance of men and women meeting as equals and participating as equals in all social and public spaces. They have gone on record against the idea of separate family or divorce courts for different religious communities and are no less opposed to single-sex education.

For readers encountering Ni Putes Ni Soumises for the first time, the various elements that have gone into the making of the movement may challenge expectations, and the reasons for that are multiple and complex. Perhaps first and foremost, the writings produced by the movement have been generated in an activist rather than a theoretical context and bear almost no reference to the forms of theory most familiar in an Anglophone context. There can be little doubt that the movement contradicts received notions of the main concerns and orientation of French feminism. For more than three decades, theories of difference, variously informed by psychoanalysis, poststructuralism, and deconstruction, have dominated the French feminist scholarship most commonly imported to North American and other English-speaking universities. Thus, while early feminist claims may have benefited from notions of equality and appeals to universal rights, contemporary students of French feminism have been trained to sniff out the various biases lurking behind the all-inclusive veneer of the Rights of Man. For those familiar with the French feminist writings of Luce Irigaray, Hélène Cixous, or Julia Kristeva—all champions of difference—Ni Putes Ni Soumises may well seem historically out of joint. The movement has more in common, in some respects, with postcolonial feminisms and with feminist thought produced by women of color in the Anglophone world. But even here, NPNS challenges both the efficacy and the desirability of the discourses of difference and identity that have informed most theorizing around new left social movements and postcolonialism in Anglophone contexts.

Just as the English-speaking student of French learns to be wary of "false friends"—words that sound the same in both languages but have quite different meanings—care has to be taken with respect to cognate phenomena that appear similar on the surface but need to be understood in light of different histories, different social and political contexts and understandings, and different cultural, religious, and national practices and debates. While the difficulties facing the women represented by Ni Putes Ni Soumises are related to those faced by racial and religious minorities in the United States, for example, they are not identical to any single American counterpart. Cutting some of the organization's most publicized positions out of their complex field of intervention and pasting them into our own tradition of multiculturalism will inevitably yield puzzling and potentially misleading results. The group has certainly earned both fervent support and heated opposition on home soil, and situating Ni Putes Ni Soumises within its particular geographical and historical context may not make the organization any less controversial, but it will render the movement's positions that much more intelligible.

In moving toward a fuller understanding of how context makes a difference, consider a single example, although a central one: readers familiar with American press coverage of the veil affair and the urban riots in France might anticipate the use of certain terms to define the type of women whom NPNS represents: Arab women, Muslim women, second-generation immigrants, or economically and socially disadvantaged women. It must be noted, however, that in her writings Amara generally forgoes these designations in favor of the term "women of the *quartiers*." The French term *quartiers* simply means "neighborhoods." What, then, is the factor that serves as a common experience among residents of certain French neighborhoods and distinguishes them from other social groups? Is it simply a question of economic class? Has a group formed around distinctive religious or cultural practices? Do the members of this group self-identify with a certain ethnicity, or are they united by a collective sense of oppression as targets of racist discourse? When further qualifying the social forces that distinguish the neighborhoods in question from other French neighborhoods, Amara's vocabulary shifts, refusing to settle on any single defining condition or qualification. At times, she mentions "working-class" neighborhoods; at other moments, she alludes to the biographical details that shaped her own perspective on life in these neighborhoods—her parents' experiences of immigration from the region of Kabylia in northern Algeria, her identification as an Arab woman, and her adherence to Islam. At other times, she speaks of disadvantaged neighborhoods, of neighborhoods isolated from the city centers and lacking social and public services. The flexible character of Amara's vocabulary reflects the context of her intervention: namely, the fact that residents of these French neighborhoods have found themselves on particularly slippery discursive terrain.

While it would be tempting, especially in an American context, to present NPNS in a context that emphasizes race, religion, or even violence against women, the movement and, more particularly, its brand of activism and the positions it has taken are better understood in terms of the history of immigration in France. Before we elaborate upon current-day repercussions of France's "immigration problem," it has to be noted that foreigners residing in France were once met with a very different attitude. Faced with demographic decline in the first decades of the twentieth century, French officials welcomed mass immigration from both Europe and abroad, considering it crucial to reinforce economic growth and "create a certain breathing space in the labour market."[1] Very early in the century, political discourse surrounding the status of foreign citizens in France was almost indistinguishable from an economic discourse regarding the labor force. Although European governments were responsible for broadly sketching diplomatic relations relating to immigration, the actual recruitment of foreign workers took place through a special private organization, the Société générale d'immigration. This private enterprise also began aggressively recruiting workers from French colonies. Workers from French North Africa became especially important for the mining industry, where working conditions were so unfavorable that local recruitment efforts yielded few results.

1. This comment came from then prime minister Georges Pompidou's 1963 formulation of the economic importance of immigration. Cited in C.-V. Marie, "Entre économie et politique: Le 'clandestine,' une figure sociale à géométrie variable," *Pouvoirs* 47 (1988): 75–99.

The early relegation of immigration issues to the private labor market had several consequences. One of the most important for our current concerns is that housing accommodations for foreign workers were left entirely to the discretion of private employers. The actual solutions varied. Some companies arranged for homestays with local host families, while others provided dormitory-like living quarters for their workers. In many cases, however, workers were left entirely to their own devices, a policy that resulted in temporary, makeshift shantytowns, or *bidonvilles*, with some of these sites developing into the modern-day government housing projects that have lately earned so much media attention.

There is already a sense that several discursive fields are beginning to overlap. The figure of a foreign-born worker living in a particular type of neighborhood emerges where national origin, economic function, and urban geography intersect to form a particular configuration. Despite the glowing reception of this figure as an abstract component of the labor force, some French policy-makers began expressing anxiety about these purveyors of foreign cultural practice. While efforts to encourage assimilation do not necessarily arise from racism, it is worth noting that notions of race were not entirely absent from early concerns about cultural integration. In 1937, the demographer Georges Mauco, who would later be appointed to the Haut comité consultatif de la population et de la famille, wrote that some foreign workers currently living in France—notably Asians, Africans, and those originating from the Levant—"belong to races so different" that their "assimilation is impossible, and moreover, very often physically and morally undesirable."[2] Mauco's attitude does not represent anything like a consensus among either policy-makers or the French public; indeed, his later recommendation to impose a system of selective immigration based on his hierarchy of desirability was rejected. However, his comments serve to illustrate two points. The first is that although immigration early in the century was multiethnic, and foreign workers of both European and non-European provenance may have shared a formal political status and a common economic situation, the public's anxiety about cultural threat did not affect all immigrants equally. Additionally, Mauco's conflation of cultural assimilability with physical and moral desirability indicates that discourses of cultural difference were not entirely separate from assertions of racial difference in some arenas of French discourse. Public rhetoric mapped notions of culture and race onto the figure of the foreign worker as two representations of difference that were neither entirely identical nor entirely distinct.

2. Cited in Patrick Weil, "Racisme et discrimination dans la politique française de l'immigration 1938–1945/1974–1995," *Vingtième Siècle: Revue d'histoire* 47 (1995): 77–102.

Gender played an implicit role in this image of the foreign worker who is economically integral to France and yet potentially unassimilable from a cultural standpoint. As long as French officials imagined that able-bodied men would come to France to provide temporary "man-power" before returning to their families in their countries of origin, public anxiety about these workers' cultural mores could be held at bay. However, by midcentury, this image of the temporary, masculine worker became increasingly unconvincing. During the postwar period, the violent process of decolonization was accompanied both by an influx of people from former French colonies and by a highly politicized debate within France that affected the social reception of these populations. The Algerian war provides a particularly compelling example on both fronts. Shortly after the Second World War, the "Muslim Frenchmen of Algeria" were granted full French citizenship and thus permitted free circulation across the two banks of the Mediterranean. As a result, Algerian émigrés came to France in record numbers, fleeing economic devastation and political oppression as tensions between colonists and the independence movement mounted. While all "Frenchmen" now shared an equal juridical status, recent scholarship has suggested that institutions such as the Labor Ministry and the police force maintained practices that discriminated between the "Muslim French" and those deemed just plain "French."[3] As the violence mounted during the War of Algerian Independence, French citizens of Algerian descent were framed either as victims of police repression or as threats to national security, depending upon the sympathies of the increasingly divided French public. On October 17, 1961, protesters associated with the French branch of the Algerian independence party, the Front de libération nationale (National Front), demonstrated after the Parisian prefecture pursued measures to prevent Algerians from circulating in the streets of the capital after dark. The Paris police were given *carte blanche*, and the protesters were met with excessively violent force. The incident indicates how ambivalently the French public welcomed the postwar beneficiaries of formal French citizenship.

While the reframing of immigration in terms of national security may have relaxed a bit as peace agreements were signed following the decolonization of France's remaining colonies, perceptions of social threat remained as economic growth in France began to stall. When the country experienced a period of economic recession provoked by the oil crisis of 1973, unemployment simultaneously reduced the need for foreign labor and exacerbated

3. See Emmanuel Blanchard, "La Préfecture de police et les Algériens à Paris (1944–1956): Entre égalité des droits et situation coloniale," in *Histoire de l'immigration et question coloniale en France*, ed. Nancy L. Green and Marie Poinsot (Paris: La Documentation française, 2006), 51–57.

attitudes of xenophobia. Immigrants often served as a scapegoat for those affected by layoffs. In 1974, the French secretary of state for immigration halted labor migration as a result of economic pressure and cultural anxiety.

It is in this climate that the figure of the immigrant woman enters the space of public discourse. When the recruitment of foreign "man-power" was officially terminated, public debate turned to the migration of women. Immediately following the 1974 decision, the government also considered ending immigration for the purposes of "family reunification" before a public outcry blocked this measure. If reunification changed the face of immigration in terms of public discourse, it was a blessing that cut both ways as far as women were concerned. On the one hand, it brought visibility to a process now described as the "feminization of immigration." On the other hand, women became visible primarily as the companions of men already residing in France. The idea that women could neutralize the threat of cultural difference by encouraging foreign workers to "settle down" and assimilate served as a common yet backhanded argument in favor of allowing women's migration.

To the extent that France recognized the social role of foreign-born women by assigning them the task of assimilation, these women duly fulfilled their function. However, members of the following generation responded to the ambivalent reception of their mothers with an equally ambivalent attitude toward French society. By the 1980s, there was an important presence of second-generation immigrants, children born in France who not only attended French public schools but also succeeded in the French educational system. This was a generation familiar with traditional republican values and well aware of the rights and responsibilities associated with French citizenship. While this degree of assimilation seemed to deliver exactly what many French officials were hoping for, the successful education of this generation had some unexpected consequences. The children of immigrants actually turned the tools of the Republic against the very elements of public discourse that marked them as different. If the educational success of second-generation immigrants did not guarantee equal employment or protection from discrimination, it did position them to contest their situation while appealing to traditional republican values. Additionally, in October 1981, legislators overturned a century-old law that barred foreigners from forming organizations with full recognition and financial support from the French government. If this new generation was culturally prepared to fight French discrimination with the country's own ideological weapons, this legislative measure provided the concrete conditions necessary for recognition within the formal policy-making system.

Shortly afterward, the March of the Beurs set the tone for this new generation prepared to fight French discrimination on the Republic's own turf. After urban riots on the outskirts of Lyons, a small group of activists developed the idea of a long march, inspired by the work of Martin Luther King and Mahatma Gandhi. In September 1983, the march set out from Lyons toward Paris with two simple aims: to obtain ten-year residence permits and the right to vote for foreigners living on French soil. The marchers began rapidly picking up momentum as they progressed from neighborhood to neighborhood, so that by December, ten thousand people demonstrated in the streets of Paris under the banner of republican values—liberty, equality, and fraternity. Well-established organizations representing immigrant rights, union organizers, and seasoned activists came out to support the marchers, but the most significant show of support came from the youth collectives who were demonstrating for the first time. Although the march had begun in Lyons with two specific demands, it had clearly mobilized something much broader by the time it arrived in Paris: a new generation had begun to develop its political voice.

In positive terms, the March of the Beurs gave youth movements the opportunity to reframe the context of their intervention. There was a sense of rupture with older social groups that framed their struggle, either in economic terms through union activity or as focused primarily on international policies concerning their nation of origin. This march's insistence on traditional French republican values reinscribed their struggle *within,* rather than in opposition to, domestic political institutions. Depending on the ideological inclinations of those marked by social and economic exclusion, this move signaled either the success of the marchers' strategy or the neutralization and co-optation of a potential force of change now in service of the status quo. Additionally, the march, which primarily featured youth of North African descent and was less well attended by those of Spanish, Portuguese, Italian, sub-Saharan, or Asian descent, positioned the "Beur" as the most visible figure of this "second generation." The term *beur* is derived from the youth practice of *verlan,* a slang form of speech that inverts the syllables of a word, in this case the French word *arabe.* The word began as a self-assigned identity category circulating among the French-born descendants of North African immigrants. However, the media quickly co-opted the term and employed it to describe the community from the outside. The ambiguous politics of the term's usage aptly reflect the general consequences of shifting the debate over immigration to the terrain of ethnic specificity. This move permitted youth of a particular background to unite not only around political claims but also around a set of common cultural and social practices. At the same time, however, it allowed the general French public to reduce the economic and political issues facing the most disadvantaged neighborhoods to notions of religious, ethnic, and perhaps even racial differences.

In order to capitalize upon the success of the first march, a second march was planned the following year. Officially sponsored by the Collectif des jeunes issus de l'immigration, demonstrators rallied in five cities across France to protest discrimination and racism. While the first march had established a loose consensus among youth eager to articulate a new political direction, the second incited heated internal debates about what that direction might be. While several activist organizations were founded in the aftermath of this second march in 1984, two in particular emerged at the national level as the most visible representatives of two divergent views. The first organization, SOS Racisme, focused on challenging racist and xenophobic attitudes. The movement was racially mixed and made its claims through a universalist discourse. The second, France-Plus, formulated a discourse that did not shy away from ethnic specificity, and thus concentrated its efforts on concrete political representation for France's ethnically distinct communities. While certainly not the only voices of social change in France at the time, these two approaches reflect two different lines of thought. In order to combat social attitudes justifying racism and xenophobia, SOS Racisme focused its claims in the domain of abstract, universal citizenship. By contrast, France-Plus appealed to arguments of ethnic or cultural specificity in order to make its case for political representation of this newly articulated collective.

While the two organizations were often in conflict, their different approaches contributed to several common achievements. The first was to appropriate and redefine French notions of citizenship. Their combined efforts not only gave France's traditional political institutions a more multiethnic face but also created new avenues for political participation, notably through local nonprofit organizations and grassroots activism. On the other hand, the very achievements of these organizations also presented difficulties for subsequent generations of activists. One consequence was the establishment of certain media "stars" who quickly rose to the forefront of public debate. It was the strength of this "second generation" of activists—their familiarity with the national political system and their dedication to republican values—that made them palatable to a more general French public, marketable for the media, and easily assimilated into mainstream political institutions. This, of course, lent itself to the sentiment among many that these same media stars had at best become removed from, and at worst betrayed, their grassroots origins. At the same time, the fact that the most vocal representatives of this "second generation" were of North African origin rallying under the title of

"Beur" inadvertently reinforced discriminatory notions of difference at a time when the French public was beginning to perceive social problems in more racial or ethnically particular terms.

In 1989, the first of a succession of French "veil affairs" hit the media. Three junior high school–age students refused to return to school after their principal, citing the French tradition of *laïcité*, prohibited them from wearing veils on campus.[4] The series of publicized reactions that ensued placed young Muslim women at the center of debates over integration, discrimination, and social cohesion. Once again, anxiety about cultural assimilability was mapped onto the figure of immigrant women. This time, however, the contradictions internal to the Beur movement complicated the struggle over these women's dress. The republican ideal of abstract equality, religious neutrality, and race-blind citizenship conflicted with certain conceptions of recognition. Which discourse would best protect these young women? One that would assert their choice as individuals at the risk of reinforcing xenophobic perceptions of otherness, or one that would protect the school as a neutral public sphere at the risk of forcing minority groups to assimilate to dominant cultural norms?

In light of both the gains and the challenges of the Beur movement, activists in the following decade were left with muddy terrain to navigate. Communitarianism (*communautarisme*) became a watchword in French social discourse. For some, the idea of rallying behind a certain set of cultural,

4. *Laïcité* is the French conception of secularism and generally refers to the separation of church and state, but the history behind it differentiates it enough from its English counterparts that we have where possible left the term in the original French to mark this difference. Whereas the American notion of secularism grew out of the need to ensure religious freedoms and to protect religious groups from state interference, in part by preventing any single religious denomination or group from becoming the state religion, the French notion was intended to ensure citizens' primary allegiance to the state rather than the church (in this case, the Catholic Church and pope). As such, *laïcité* insists on the relegation of religion to the private sphere and expresses the state's intent not only to protect individuals from the claims of religion but also to protect public spaces from religious interference and dominance. In short, while American secularism is freedom *of* religion and religious practice, French secularism is better cast as freedom *from* religion and religious practice. Furthermore, although *laïcité* began as a negative prohibition on religion in the realm of the state, today it also serves as a kind of positive horizon or as an ideal of uniting people of different religious convictions within a single inclusive social and political society. In this latter sense, it connotes a process that cannot be achieved in a single moment or by a single decree. For a fuller discussion of *laïcité*, especially in its connections with France's various headscarf affairs, see Bronwyn Winter, *Hijab and the Republic: Uncovering the French Headscarf Debate* (Syracuse: Syracuse University Press, 2008); and Joan Wallach Scott, *The Politics of the Veil* (Princeton: Princeton University Press, 2007).

religious, or ethnic affinities seemed to provide the best way to correct for the concrete problems that the abstract discourse of universalism had left untouched. Groups suffering from a particular type of oppression could articulate that common experience and bring visibility to those issues. At the same time, others complained that the very causes that the Beur movement had so successfully defended at the beginning—antiracism, social and political equality, an appropriation of traditional republican values—had been undermined. The charge of communitarianism—suggesting an insular identity-based politics—was employed to call attention to the dangers of political balkanization and the potential racialization of the issues facing France's multiethnic neighborhoods and the multinational history of immigration. For those following that line of thought, the fragmentation of this well-assimilated multiethnic generation into distinct ethnic, religious, or cultural groups represented a step backward rather than a step forward.

Another consequence of the Beur movement's assimilation within the traditional institutional framework was that many organizations became increasingly dependent on political parties or existing political institutions. On the one hand, this permitted organizations representing second-generation youth to benefit from both the financial resources and the public legitimacy that are so important to the traditional path of long-term viability for many French social movements. On the other hand, it brought anxieties that these organizations would be restricted, co-opted, or even made to serve the interests of the status quo. As a different yet related concern, the cooperation of many grassroots movements with more mainstream institutions also ran the risk of relegating the management of social problems to local, grassroots organizations rather than forcing the French government to address the issues facing its most vulnerable citizens.

These anxieties about communitarianism, coupled with the increased cooperation of grassroots movements with mainstream political institutions, raised fears of colonial-style "partnership." Under the notorious "Indigenous Codes," colonized peoples had been considered French subjects without being French citizens. Subject to French rule without enjoying the rights and responsibilities of the French citizen, the colonized were relegated to special tribunals that conferred justice according to local "custom" as interpreted by a few indigenous elites designated by the colonial authorities. The trend of allowing local organizations to provide social services and "handle" the populations of the *banlieues* themselves, and charging them (whether explicitly or implicitly) with the task of diffusing upheaval and neutralizing the "threat to security," began to look suspiciously like the colonial system of managing subjugated populations. In light of France's particular colonial past, terms such as "grassroots politics," "multiculturalism," and "self-governance" did not sound so innocent to many French ears.

While this history of issues affecting residents of the *quartiers* throughout the twentieth century is by no means exhaustive, it does give the reader a sense of the complex domain of public discourse in which Amara grew up and which she faced as she developed her own public voice. Throughout the 1990s, activists began planning a new phase of social intervention capable of responding to the Beur movement's successes and problems during the preceding decade. Aware of the dangers of co-optation and the "media star" system, many began focusing their energies on more concrete, local struggles. This period witnessed the emergence of several organizations dedicated to resolving social issues specific to a single neighborhood while emphasizing a certain degree of political independence in order to bypass traditional left-right divides. If the ideological positions of the Beur generation's most prominent figures had helped in tackling attitudes at the national level, this new wave of organizations adopted a more pragmatic approach. While universalist values and recognition of difference might be antagonistic on an abstract level, they might be successfully combined to address more specific, concrete issues. Organizations were founded to address the fight against drugs (Espoir Goutte d'Or) and to promote culture and sports in low-income neighborhoods (EPI, sport et culture). It is under this rubric that feminist organizations began cropping up to address the specificity of women's experiences in low-income neighborhoods (Nahda, Nanas Beurs, Femmes des Francs-Moisins). Although these tendencies may loosely describe a new wave of activism, they by no means suggest a complete rupture with past forms and organizations. In fact, readers will recognize the lasting impact of former activist intervention upon the development of Ni Putes Ni Soumises.

Fadela Amara's personal trajectory suggests the extent to which earlier Beur movements shaped her political perspectives as well as her tactical decisions. At the age of seventeen, Amara began working locally in her housing project at Clermont-Ferrand to secure political representation for the multiethnic youth of her neighborhood. Her earliest activities, including a local civic march to get youth from her neighborhood on electoral ballots, reflect the institutional, directly political approach that became the hallmark of this second generation so at home with the internal political functioning of France. If the first March of the Beurs alerted her to her generation's potential, it was the second march that alerted her to the tensions that the Beur generation would have to address. Faced with the conflicting visions of a specifically Beur movement versus a multiethnic movement of French solidarity, it was the latter that seemed most promising to Amara. Like many youth in her position during the 1980s, she was drawn to SOS Racisme by the image of "Blacks, Whites, and Beurs" marching together in solidarity. When SOS Racisme founded a sister organization, the Maison des potes, in 1988, Amara became an activist employed full-time there. The Maison des potes sought to contest the negative images of the *banlieues* that had gained currency in public opinion by promoting positive initiatives such as large neighborhood dinners, akin to American block parties.

As early as 1989, Amara led a women's commission at her local branch of the Maison des potes in Clermont-Ferrand, looking into the effect of ghettoization and ethnic discrimination specifically as it pertained to young women. Throughout the nineties, a series of conditions exacerbated the situation of gender inequality in France's most marginalized neighborhoods and increased the need for intervention. The most sensational acts of gender violence that were reported are only the effects of this rapid deterioration of living conditions in the *quartiers*. Amara gives a nuanced analysis of the interlocking causes in the text of this book. For our current purposes, it will suffice to say that the indications of increased gender violence were compelling enough that by 2000 the Maison des potes placed Amara in the national office in order to expand her inquiry into women's situations in the *quartiers*.

It is significant that one of Amara's first initiatives was to organize a seminar for women of the *quartiers* to learn about feminism. At the time, the relationship between these women's struggles and the history of French feminism was far from obvious for several reasons. Many of the claims of contemporary mainstream feminists appeared removed from the most pressing concerns in the *quartiers*. Attempts to break the glass ceiling hardly resonated in neighborhoods devastated by poverty and unemployment. Likewise, as the French government reduced state funding in low-income neighborhoods, the struggle for gender parity among politicians seemed far removed from the concerns of populations with little access to public services, let alone effective political representation. This does not mean that women of the *quartiers* were unaware of the way that economic and political exclusion affected gender relationships. A common attitude, however, was that discrimination and poverty were the more pressing issues; perhaps if general forms of oppression could be alleviated, then women's oppression would follow suit.

One of Amara's early insights was the need to turn that formulation on its head. She imagined that women's situation could serve as a privileged vantage point to address the entire political context affecting the *quartiers*. This approach is consistent, of course, with the general climate of activism following the Beur movement: start with a specific, local issue and work outward. The idea was to begin with women's concrete concerns. From the intersection where notions of culture, race, and class have historically been mapped onto these women's bodies, a course could be plotted to contest more general conditions affecting the *quartiers.* Amara was not the only person to recognize the potential of this approach. Approximately eighty people, both boys and girls, attended her seminar on feminism, and together they produced a four-hundred-page dossier outlining the history of feminism, from the suffragettes to the struggle for access to abortion. The dossier also includes information on American feminist struggles. While readers may certainly recognize affinities between the movement's rhetoric and other feminisms, it is important to remember that the *quartier* youth initially had an uneasy relationship to prior feminist struggles. As Amara describes it, feminism was a discovery for the most recent generation of *quartier* activists, not a birthright. Those who attended the first seminar saw it as a rich history to be mined and appropriated, but their eventual intervention into that tradition was not predetermined or ready-made.

As Amara and her commission began orienting themselves within that tradition, one of their first decisions was to adopt a universalist position emphasizing equality and cooperation among the sexes, distancing themselves from the theories of difference that had become popular in France since the 1970s. While an emphasis on gender specificity and the establishment of all-women safe spaces may have been effective strategies in preceding decades, many women of the *quartiers* judged this approach unwise in the context of their current situation. The risk of igniting a "war between the sexes" in a climate that was becoming increasingly tense with sectarian animosity was too great. From the very beginning, Amara's commission emphasized the participation of both men and women in organizing events and an atmosphere of mutual respect among youth: *mixité* would become a core value of the NPNS movement.[5] Amara would continue to be wary not only of policies that encourage divisiveness between genders, but also of claims that might encourage divisions along ethnic or class lines. Throughout her career as an activist, she has been critical of those feminist struggles she deems "private"

5. *Mixité* is commonly used in French to refer to the coexistence of men and women in a shared space, whether for work, education, leisure, or social or political projects. Unlike many feminist organizations in France, NPNS has been a mixed organization from its inception, and one of its central concerns is that women and men meet in all spheres of life as social and political equals. The term is also sometimes used to refer to the coexistence of different ethnic groups or social classes. In general, *mixité* demands that different groups mix, cooperate, and interact in the same social space.

struggles, those issues where primarily upper- or middle-class women would stand to gain. In many respects, this stance is comparable to the criticisms launched by African American feminists against the largely white, bourgeois feminist movement in the seventies and eighties.

In the autumn of 2001, Amara and fellow activists organized a series of local assemblies in neighborhoods across the country to gather information. Once the silence was broken, the results were so astounding that the organizers decided to distribute a questionnaire in order to prepare a more formal analysis of the situation before a Special Assembly in Paris. The organizers received more than five thousand completed questionnaires, and the sociologist Hélène Orain compiled the responses in the "White Book," a document included in this volume and testifying to the concerns facing women at the beginning of the millennium. After the findings were discussed at the Special Assembly, which took place in January 2002, the women in attendance prepared a manifesto outlining specific demands for elected officials. However, reactions from politicians were scarce. It became clear that activists concerned about gender in the *banlieues* would have to take additional steps in order to get their issues on the official agenda of candidates and major political parties.

The urgency of the White Book's findings was underscored by the particularly appalling crime perpetrated against Sohane Benziane, a seventeen-year-old girl who was burned alive in the Balzac housing projects of Vitry-sur-Seine by an enemy of her teenage boyfriend.[6] Sohane's death raised awareness of gender violence in France's low-income neighborhoods and reinforced the demands for immediate intervention. It was shortly after this event that Fadela Amara and six young activists, women and men alike, led their first initiative, the March of Women against the Ghetto and for Equality. From February 1 to March 8, 2003, this small group traveled to twenty-three cities across France, seeking to meet with local officials and holding meetings in various housing projects to address difficult issues relating to sexuality, gang rape, discrimination, gender violence, ghettoization, religion and public secularism, extremism, forced marriage, and republican values in an increasingly

6. Sohane's sister Kahina gave an interview to *Elle* magazine in which she discusses the facts of her sister's death and her own need to speak out against the treatment of women in France's housing projects. See "La révolte de Kahina," *Elle*, February 2003, 53–55. Sohane's attacker, Jamal Derrar, was convicted of torture and barbarity leading to unintended death and sentenced to twenty-five years in prison. Another man was sentenced to eight years for having barred the door during the attack. "French Man Jailed in Torture Case," BBC News, April 8, 2006, http://news.bbc.co.uk/2/hi/europe/4891474.stm (accessed August 15, 2010).

divided society. As the march swung through the south of France, in cities with the largest immigrant populations, local media coverage brought increasing attention, and the events the group staged began drawing hundreds of attendees rather than just handfuls. By the time the march reached its final destination in Paris, on May 8, International Women's Day, an estimated thirty thousand protesters came out to demonstrate under the banner "Ni Putes Ni Soumises." In the months following the astonishing success of the march, the slogan was converted to the title of a permanent organization so that the momentum could be translated into concrete action.

In its first months, the newly created Ni Putes Ni Soumises organization signaled an approach that would synthesize both direct political intervention and a dedication to changing social and cultural attitudes. The prime minister at the time, Jean-Pierre Raffarin, received representatives of the organization, and the movement was invited to join the official celebration of French independence on July 14, 2003. Through an initiative titled "Today's Mariannes," portraits of fourteen women of all ethnicities dressed as Marianne, the symbolic protectress of French republican values, were hung on the front columns of the building housing France's National Assembly. The portraits were by turns beautiful, whimsical, and lyrical, and the exhibit as a whole was aesthetically stunning. The exhibition suggested a challenge to public opinion at the cultural level, an appropriation of the space of traditional policy-making institutions by France's multiethnic youth, and an awareness of how the specific issue of gender figures into symbolic representations of republican rights and values.

In the months following the initial success of Ni Putes Ni Soumises, however, the organization's initiatives were far from merely symbolic. Many of its activities testify to the concrete action that is so important to the third generation. Goaded by the marchers' meeting with Raffarin and the march's early media attention, the French government accepted and adopted five of the initiatives proposed in the Ni Putes Ni Soumises petition. Among them was funding for a *Guide to Respect*, a manual distributed to students of middle and high school age emphasizing equality between the sexes and individual decision making in issues pertaining to sexuality, intimate relationships, and family life. Funding was also appropriated for a center that would serve simultaneously as a neighborhood drop-in resource center and the headquarters of the movement. Today the national office of NPNS in the 20th arrondissement of Paris is staffed by a legal expert and two volunteer psychologists, who are available to anyone in need of counsel. The staff also runs a yearly educational event called Université Ni Putes Ni Soumises, which organizes seminars, cultural events, and protests to raise awareness about women's issues; it regularly attracts four to five hundred participants. In recent years, the organization has expanded its activities at the international level. In addition to the twenty-three committees within French territory that represent Ni Putes Ni Soumises locally, four additional committees represent the organization in other European countries. The group also formed numerous partnerships abroad, notably one with an organization that promotes the education of young women in rural Morocco. When the United Nations formally recognized Ni Putes Ni Soumises in 2007, it became clear that the movement's message resonated beyond French borders.

In the spring of 2007, Amara made headlines again when she accepted a post as Secrétaire d'Etat chargée de la politique de la ville (minister of urban policy) in the government of Nicolas Sarkozy and François Fillon. Her appointment was one of several that were hailed, by right- and left-leaning media alike (and often with overt suspicion), as an opening toward "diversity" in the new government. To some, Amara's appointment looked to be a shrewd calculation on the part of the Sarkozy government: if she could improve conditions in the *quartiers*, then so much the better; and if she was unable to, then the Sarkozy administration could point to their minister from the *quartiers* and say they had done their best. To others, Amara's acceptance of the position has seemed just as calculated. Inside the NPNS organization, Amara's move generated heated controversy, with some expressing concern about the future of the movement and others proclaiming that Fadela Amara was not NPNS and that her personal choice did not affect the organization one way or the other. Still others felt that Fadela had betrayed her own and the movement's leftist roots in agreeing to work with Sarkozy's rightist government. Speculation regarding Amara's tenure as minister only intensified in 2010 when the president removed her from her post. This occurred as part of a cabinet reshuffle that targeted many of the leftists and racial minorities who had once signaled a gesture toward ethnic and political diversity under Sarkozy's regime. Today the movement continues under the leadership of Sihem Habchi, somewhat less controversially than it did at its inception and under Amara's leadership, but with much the same message and strategies of intervention.

The texts included in this volume span the most dynamic years of the movement, from its inception in 2002 to Amara's departure in 2007. The first selection contains four documents that were assembled and presented to participants at the États géneraux de femmes des quartiers, or Special Assembly of Women of the *Quartiers*—the meeting convened by Amara in her capacity as president of the Maison des potes. The "White Book" is the longest and most important of these documents and includes firsthand testimony by women from the *quartiers* who responded to a survey and participated in the local meetings that led up to the Special Assembly. The text interweaves firsthand accounts with a more general analysis of the conditions and problems facing women in the *quartiers*. Topics range from women's participation in local and national politics to urban violence, racism, educational opportunities and pink collar jobs, the direct control of young women's choices (from what to wear to going out at night), gender equality within the family, and oppressive cultural practices such as polygamy, excision, and forced marriage. Without mentioning it by name, the presentation of issues in the White Book is a model of intersectional analysis, showing that women's lives and the problems they face are shaped not only by sex and gender, but by the intersection of these with class, race, ethnicity, and the history of colonization. And here in this early statement, as in all of the movement's later writings, the focus is not simply on improving women's lot, but on lifting the whole community. As the manifesto included in these documents puts it, "Life in the *quartiers*, for the families who live there, for the children and their future, will not change unless we women regain our place and our dignity."

The second section of the book translates nine chapters from *Scum of the Republic*, Amara's second book, coauthored with the then secretary-general of NPNS, Mohammed Abdi.[7] The book was published in France one year after the 2005 riots. The title bears reference to an exchange between a bystander and Nicolas Sarkozy, then minister of the interior, during the latter's visit to Argenteuil during the riots. Responding to a woman standing on a balcony

7. Fadela Amara and Mohammed Abdi, *La racaille de la République* (Paris: Éditions du Seuil, 2006). The basic structure of *Racaille* is in many respects parallel to the structure of Amara's first book, written with Sylvia Zappi and titled simply *Ni Putes Ni Soumises* (Paris: La Découverte, 2003). Both books begin autobiographically, although the account in *Racaille* is twice as long as the earlier one, then move into a more general reflection on social issues. What Amara writes in the opening lines of *Ni Putes Ni Soumises* could stand at the head of all she writes: "My own personal history has undoubtedly shaped the way I analyze the situation of women" (13). But whereas the earlier book focuses mainly on giving a firsthand account of the conditions facing women in the *cités* and *banlieues*, and then showing how the movement grew out of those conditions and experiences, *Racaille* positions itself more explicitly as a mature piece of social analysis and commentary. The same themes occur in both books, but in *Racaille* the perspective is broader and more explicitly aimed at influencing local and national policy. The earlier book, *Ni Putes Ni Soumises*, has been translated into English as *Breaking the Silence: French Women's Voices from the Ghetto* (Berkeley: University of California Press, 2006).

several stories above him, Sarkozy said reassuringly, "We will rid you of this scum." Widely reported in the media, the comment was said to have fueled further rioting, and was condemned as racist.[8] Sarkozy defended himself, not only saying that no word in the rich French language should be off limits, but also adding that he was only using a phrase that the woman herself had used first. Amara and Abdi's book is not a direct retort to Sarkozy, but suggests that here the so-called "scum" would like the chance to speak up on their own behalf. We have translated those sections of the book in which Amara and Abdi share their respective life stories and discuss their views and analysis of pressing social issues such as immigration, integration, discrimination, the need for equality, the right to safety, social violence, and their hopes for France's future. As the book appeared in the lead-up to France's presidential election of 2007, it also contained reflections on the candidates and their positions. We have omitted those sections and other material in the original that seemed too limited to the French context of its publication.

Finally, we conclude this book with an interview conducted with Fadela Amara over two days in July 2007. Amara had just then left NPNS to become France's junior minister of urban policy, and we met with her in her new offices in the 7th arrondissement. With a frescoed map of the French colonies on her oval office wall and a view of the Champs du Mars and the Eiffel Tower outside, it was a far cry from the renovated supermarket building that served as the national office of NPNS. In our questions, which Amara answered without hesitation, we asked her to look back on where the NPNS movement came from, to reflect on some of its most controversial stands, and to look forward to the work she would do in her new position. We would like to thank Fadela Amara for her generosity in making time for this interview during a very busy

8. The proper English translation of *racaille* was also debated. The British daily the *Guardian* originally translated the word as "scum" but then chose to adopt the less inflammatory "rabble." Neither term is quite adequate, the former being somewhat stronger than the word's use in ordinary everyday French, the latter sounding antiquated in English. In 2002 Azouz Begag, then the minister in charge of equal opportunity policies, used the term to refer to young people who flouted the law, rode motor scooters on the sidewalk, and generally frightened the rest of the population. Laurent Greilsamer of *Le Monde* notes that in the 1873 *Littré* dictionary, the word was described as harsher than "scoundrel" (*canaille*) and notes that Sarkozy's use of the term managed in one fell stroke to return to the word to its most incendiary meaning. Political commentator Doug Ireland described *racaille* in the context in which Sarkozy used it as more pejorative than "scum" because it was meant to designate a whole class of people as subhuman. See the blog post "Inflammatory Language," http://www.guardian.co.uk/news/blog/2005/nov/08/inflammatoryla (accessed August 13, 2010).

period of transition. Equally deserving of our thanks are Mohammed Abdi, Sihem Habchi, and the staff at the Maison de la mixité in Paris for their support of this project and for their time and assistance in helping us to understand the movement and its significance. For help and encouragement at various points in the process, we would also like to thank Florence Faucher-King, Peg Simons, Eric Touya, Tiffany Florvil, our anonymous reviewers, and Joan Catapano, our editor at the University of Illinois Press. Special thanks are due to Joe Mai, Martin Walter, and Jane Lyle, whose generous help improved this translation considerably.

Part I

Breaking Ground

The Special Assembly of Women of the *Quartiers*

Women of the *Quartiers*

A Call to Action

Every generation carries the potential to mobilize for new rights. The seventies and eighties were a fruitful time in the fight for equality and women's rights, and important advances were made. However, since the eighties, social and economic crises (especially severe in the *banlieues*), immigration and integration policies, and attempts to roll back certain rights have posed new challenges to women's place in society.

One of these new challenges is the way in which violence doubly affects women and young girls. They are the first to feel the pressures of sexism within their families, but also in society, in their everyday lives. **We think that if women and young girls in the *quartiers* are given the opportunity to assert themselves by participating in collective actions, they will play an important role in changing the *quartiers*,** in constructing new social relationships, and in their own emancipation. **We think that silence and isolation are the principal sources of oppression,** because it is impossible to face psychological, familial, or community pressures alone and impossible to battle prejudice and ignorance individually.

The National Federation of the Maisons des potes must give these women a voice and call attention to the actions that are already being taken to develop a positive model in opposition to the violence that has become the rule in the *quartiers*. The federation must be a hub for information about initiatives undertaken by women in local organizations. It must also be the public voice of those who suffer and demand their rights. Because women from the *quartiers* are often immigrants or the children of immigrants, they carry the weight of a culture that sometimes runs counter to their most fundamental legal rights as those are understood in our country. Nonetheless, without rejecting their origins and their culture, some of them are engaged with organizations and activities that fight against specific oppressions.

We think that this generational struggle, which is emerging little by little and somewhat disparately, must unite its energies and find its full expression in order to breathe new life into feminist struggles and to offer a new model for social relations in the *quartiers*.

The federation has focused its work over the past two years on the challenges facing women in the *quartiers,* activating our entire network on this question. We worked first to bring women out of their isolation, and then to create a collective process, leading finally to the National Special Assembly of Women of the *Quartiers*.

All of this work was brought together in the "White Book of the Women of the *Quartiers*," prepared for the National Special Assembly. The White Book contains both analysis of the reality in which the women of the *quartiers* live and firsthand accounts by young girls and women.

The **Special Assembly took place January 26 and 27, 2002,** at the Sorbonne and brought together more than 250 women from the *quartiers* of France. It was a tremendous success.

A **Petition** of women of the *quartiers*, titled "**Ni Putes Ni Soumises,**" was one result of the Special Assembly, and we continue to receive signatures even today.

The first objective following the Special Assembly was to publish a **"Manifesto of the Women of the *Quartiers*,"** designed to turn the attention of national candidates, as well as government institutions, toward concrete proposals to resolve the problems encountered by young girls and women in the *quartiers*.[1] The work of the National Federation of the Maisons des potes has ensured that the manifesto will have a wide distribution among interested organizations, in order to popularize its proposals and to arrive over time at significant advances in the domain of women's rights. The proposals gathered here are meant to advance the rights of women and women's

1. The 2002 presidential election in France consisted in a first-round election on April 21 and a runoff election between the top two candidates on May 5. The first-round election shocked the French public by producing a runoff between Jacques Chirac and Jean-Marie Le Pen. Le Pen's National Front Party is generally regarded by the mainstream French press and the public as being very far to the right, if not extremist, in its anti-immigration views. In the May election, Chirac won with more than 80 percent of the popular vote. —Trans.

integration into society. They concern the subjects broached over the course of the Special Assembly: violence, sexuality, education, the weight of religion, and discrimination.

The objective of this movement is to restore and ensure respect for the fundamental rights of women in the *quartiers* and to give them the necessary tools for an emancipatory process that will affirm them as full citizens.

The White Book of the Women of the *Quartiers*

Preamble

In this text we wanted to take a preliminary inventory of the living conditions of women in the *quartiers*, to be used as the basis for the talks to be held during the National Special Assembly in Paris on January 26 and 27, 2002.[1] This is in no way meant to be an exhaustive study; it is neither an official report nor a scientific inquiry. Our work is based on three sources: the questionnaires we distributed, mainly within our network; the debates of our local assemblies; and the things women said, for which we wanted to allot sufficient space in the form of testimony. For obvious reasons, most of the testimony transcribed in the following pages was left anonymous. First and foremost, we must thank all of those who contributed directly or indirectly to this text: the working group who brought together all the sources and wrote the text, the team who worked with the questionnaire results, and finally all the friends who agreed to give their testimony and who helped bring these words into existence.

1. These Special Assemblies were called *États généraux*. The term recalls the Estates General held under France's Ancient Regime, a legislative assembly representing each of the nation's three classes, or estates. Although the institution dates back to the Middle Ages, it played a particular role in the years leading up to the French Revolution. Contesting absolute monarchy, the three estates, which traditionally convened separately, united to form a National Assembly composed not of classes, but of the people as a whole. —Trans.

A profile of those who responded to the questionnaires

We received around two hundred responses:

- Many of you are single and live with your parents.
- The majority of you do not work, but that is because you have children that you take care of.
- There are also many among you who are students or who are taking courses (French classes . . .).
- The majority of you are members of an activist organization.
- You play a sport or you dance, but you would also like to play music.
- You are ready to mobilize yourselves for a number of causes (against child abuse, against racism, for the right to housing . . .).

We should say something about the title [Ni Putes Ni Soumises]. Intentionally provocative, it may shock certain people. So what? To those people, we respond that we are not things; we are proud to be women, and we refuse the stereotypes within which they would like to confine us. We are not for sale, nor are we there for the taking; we will not be submissive or docile. We are not about condemning the women who, for various reasons, are led to prostitution or who submit to violence at the hands of men. Before everything else, that has to be said.

Introduction

This text was written because women of the quartiers are fed up. We are fed up with multiple, daily attacks, with wandering hands, with psychological pressure. We are fed up with having to justify our activities every time we leave the house. We are fed up with unemployment and poverty. We are fed up with not being able to leave our houses in peace, fed up with the thugs who are ruining our lives. We are fed up with running around nonstop between kids, work, errands, household chores, and meals. We are fed up with having to hear tasteless jokes about our clothes or our friends.

Women's condition seems to have generally improved in comparison to what it was twenty years ago. We should not forget that laws pertaining to contraception, abortion, and professional equality have allowed for immense progress, progress owing to the struggles led by women themselves. Even more recently, the political parity law and improvements in family policy (paternity leave, for example) have constituted new areas of progress, even if they come nowhere close to solving everything. But it is time to recognize that the situation for many of us has deteriorated in the last ten years, when we have not purely and simply been kept at a complete distance from these measures and possibilities. For many of us, political parity had no more effect than an ad for a sale at Hermès. Would we stand for election when we lack the means do so? Who would watch our children during the meetings? Would our partners or our brothers agree to run errands or do the dishes in our place?

For parity, even if . . .
Nathalie, a young elected official who represents a banlieue near Lyons

"As an elected official, I have two disadvantages: I am young and I am a woman. From the beginning, I had to fight to be respected. I had to appear much tougher and meaner than I am in reality. It will be a long struggle to get guys to accept women in politics. But that's why I believe that parity can help, even if it's not enough on its own. I believe that women who have the chance to be politically active occupy a space that they wouldn't otherwise, and that can also change things. But of course I'm not naïve. Parity doesn't resolve the problem of childcare, of time away from household chores . . ."

There are even more serious things. Economic crisis and mass unemployment swept through our neighborhoods and challenged many of the previous gains. Women are the first victims of unemployment, financial insecurity, reduced hours, and underemployment. In the eighties, we believed that education and academic success would compensate for our difficulties. Well, we were certainly disillusioned! Many of us found ourselves working in dead-end jobs without any professional opportunities. Despite our extensive efforts to succeed at school and at college, the world of work retained its sexist values and reserved a position for us that was hardly enviable, when it was not openly hostile. The situation in the family is not much more satisfying. All the surveys show that things have not fundamentally changed: "Eight hours at the factory, five hours at the stove, women only have it good in the pages of *Vogue*!" In '68, women chanted this slogan in demonstrations. Thirty years later, what's changed? About ten minutes?

On the "New Man"

Sabrina, a mother of three

"These ads, like the ones for cleaning products where you see a guy telling his wife to take a soothing bath and relax while he takes care of everything, they're really ambiguous. On the one hand, it's a change from the image of a woman slaving away. I guess that for some couples it can encourage discussion and make guys think. But at the same time, it's not clear that it changes much concretely. It's the women who are going to buy this product that paints such a pretty picture, since with this product, even guys can do the housework."

In daily life, talk of sharing domestic chores is just lip service. Without even going so far as to demand domestic parity, we cannot ignore the appalling climate that prevails in many families in the *quartiers*. Everything is a power relation, everything comes down to violence or psychological pressure. Going out at night, choosing our clothes, everything always has to be negotiated and renegotiated. Not to mention that many things are forbidden for us (having a boyfriend, for example). In many housing projects, the weight of tradition and the influence of religion are clearly issues. And then there are public spaces. This is undoubtedly where things have deteriorated the most over the past few years. The street, the bus, and the malls have become dangerous places for us, and not just at night. We have to constantly be aware of our surroundings and keep a low profile to avoid problems. Who among us has not been insulted, followed, or attacked?

The results of our survey identified violence—ordinary, physical, psychological, or symbolic—as a primary concern. But ultimately, the most surprising thing is the silence surrounding the degradation of our living conditions and our social relationships. Week after week, the media bombards us with reports and investigations of violence and crime. Are women addressed anywhere in these reports? Never, nowhere. Even though the candidates in the next presidential election have all put security on their list of national priorities—again—there is radio silence on the topic of women. Yet three months from now, these personalities will all come to our neighborhoods to campaign and solicit our votes.

So we had to react. Reacting means first of all sharing our experiences, thinking about what each of us is living through, trying to understand what has caused our situation to deteriorate. Hence these Special Assemblies and this text. We wanted the text to be straightforward and unambiguous. It does not ignore the difficulties we encounter, nor our own resignation, which invites paternalism and oppression. It does not obscure the raw and brutal reality of the violence that has made some of us its witnesses or victims. Certain people will undoubtedly be surprised by some of the testimony. All the better. For many of us, our word is our best weapon, often our only one. We also wanted to recognize the many local initiatives, which deserve immense credit just for existing. They are diverse, and not all of them have seen tangible results. But because they show that women everywhere are fighting and mobilizing against all forms of oppression, because they contribute to constructing women's consciousness, these experiments are the first paving stones in the path to emancipation. The reality that we are presenting is one of contrasts: very dark in certain respects, more positive in others. But it is this very reality that we wanted to describe and understand in order to prepare for these Special Assemblies.

We are pursuing two objectives. The first and perhaps the most important is speaking out. For years we have been served pitiful discourses colored by condescension. These discourses say a lot about the place some people would like to grant us.

In Other People's Eyes

Najet, a journalist

"... Being a journalist was my childhood dream. I went to a private school, and so I found myself surrounded by very privileged people, whereas I was working hard. It was the first time in my life that I experienced such a stark gap. The other students gave me looks because I was of Arab descent and I came from a modest background, from a housing project. Their looks were loaded with clichés. What does she want? What is she doing here ... ? But I think the most jarring thing that happened to me was when a friend from school told me that I really deserved credit for succeeding, considering my background.

When I finished school, I told myself that if the world of journalism was what I had seen at school, then I wasn't going to make it there. It took me several years to regain that desire to become a journalist. I realized that at the beginning, in my profession, people had trouble giving me credit because I was a young woman and I come from a working-class background."

Whether it is a question of condemning us or pitying us does not matter. Nobody ever comes to ask our opinion. Everything happens as if others can speak and think for us ... That era is behind us. Not only do we have things to say, but further—an extraordinary demand—we want to be heard. That is our second objective: to confront [*interpeller*]. To confront those who govern us and who, for the most part, have no awareness of our condition. To confront the institutions that too often treat us with indifference, if not with contempt. To confront, finally, our friends, our brothers, our parents, our neighbors—to spur debates and to mobilize the women of the *quartiers*.

Victimization Is Unbearable

Fadela, the president of an organization and a political activist
"I came to political activism through the struggle against racism. I wanted this fight against prejudice, which I had been carrying on for years, to be translated into concrete action. That's why I joined a political party. But I quickly discovered a party of the old and the important. There were no young people, neither from the *quartiers* nor from anywhere else, and even fewer young people of immigrant descent. One day I was invited by the youth movement of this party to a meeting. I thought we were going to talk politics, about what we, the youth, had to say. But I actually found myself among people who just wanted to know what it's like to live in a run-down neighborhood. It was unbelievable, I felt like a native informant. The way people see us as victims is unbearable."

In the Jungle, the Lions Always Eat the Gazelles

There is a manifest contradiction in the public debate over crime, and we need to leave it behind. For years we have claimed that delinquency originates in the economic and social situation of the *quartiers*; unemployment, poverty, and the economic crisis obviously provoked the emergence of a parallel economy that allowed some to subsist, even if only through recourse to illegal means. However, we would obviously miss the reality if we limited our analysis of the shift in the *quartiers* to the effects of social crisis. Viewed from this angle, the violence often appears absurd. What do vandals get out of the vandalism and the joyrides? What good does it do to attack a teacher or a neighborhood organizer? Who benefits from the destruction of a gym or a community center?

Everywhere in France, and not only on the outskirts of large cities, neighborhoods have become ghettos. Ghettos, first of all, because the families in greatest difficulty are concentrated there. Ghettos, most of all, because the violence that prevails there is primarily self-destructive; it is turned against the rare public services that are still available there, against the inhabitants, against the activists. Ghettos, ultimately, because the most basic rights are not respected there. As a result, a prison mentality overdetermines social interactions: you close yourself up at home with double or triple locks. The relationships between families, between generations, between adolescents themselves are expressed only through conflict; the relationships that the *quartier* maintains with the outside—with the city center, with other neighborhoods, with vendors or firemen—are increasingly tense. We are like closed-off communities; we feel as though everything that comes from outside is an intolerable intrusion. It is the law of the strongest: everyone has to make it on his or her own, and above all without counting on anyone else.

To have a more close-knit cultural and social life

Several questions were asked about meeting other women: the women we cross paths with on the bus or out doing errands, the women whom we would like to meet to talk about where we came from, the women with other perspectives who could help us enrich and share our own. The responses suggested that we would like to lead a richer social and cultural life in our neighborhoods. You often mentioned your desire to pass your mother tongue on to other people. In the same way, many of you suggested that outings (arranged by organizations) could help make your lives more enjoyable. Strictly speaking, you do not feel isolated. But your responses testify to a desire for a richer social life, for more get-togethers. The isolation is definitely there, even if we do not always want to admit it.

We women are obviously the first victims of this shift. One manifestation of the ghetto is the return of traditional forms of social organization founded on machismo and patriarchy: segregation (girls on one side, boys on the other), aggressiveness and contempt, taboos and lack of sexual fulfillment, force as the only source of authority. In this context, girls become external signs of wealth, pawns, pieces of exclusive property. Those who thought they could live as free and emancipated women are accused of being whores; those who want to remain faithful to the model of the girl from a good family are treated like servants. Faced with these impossible alternatives, the majority have no choice but to lie: to sneak out to clubs, to smoke in secret, to meet their boyfriends at a cheap motel, or to make love in the backseat of a car. Our life is sordid. We are never safe. Our most basic rights are flouted daily, and everything happens amid profound indifference, as if there were nothing more to say.

The ghetto is also in our minds . . . Are women in solidarity regarding the issue of the *quartiers*?

The responses to this question are highly divided. In terms of the big picture, half of us think that the bonds of solidarity among women in the *quartiers* are strong and real. The other half find that the everyone-for-themselves mentality dominates relationships even among women. These responses are not actually surprising. As activists for organizations, we see every day that concrete bonds of mutual support exist among women in order to resolve many of the difficulties of daily life: papers, access to housing, access to rights, and so on. We are deeply invested in these bonds because it is through our structures that these bonds exist. But at the same time, we know that far too many women are forced into confinement and isolation—either because their husbands or their brothers condemn them to it or because a fear of the outside impels them to close themselves up at home. The ghetto is also in our minds . . .

The most unbelievable part of the story is that this brutal environment still manages to make us feel guilty. Some of us wanted to escape, to leave our families, never to see the *quartiers* again, to break free of confinement. With varying degrees of success, those who escaped found work elsewhere once they finished their studies. Some married and live elsewhere. For them, turning their back on the *quartier* was the only solution. They know the painful journey of those who choose this road.

Walking the Streets: She Said She Had It in Her . . .

Nabila, an activist, tells the story of one of her friends

"One day she ran off. That's where I met her. She was no older than eighteen. She'd started hanging out at night, and that's how she heard the story of her family, because people talk. She prostituted herself a bit out of spite. She said she had it in her. Because her mother's boyfriend had raped her. She said it was nothing to her and that she didn't feel love for men. But she was actually devaluing herself. The reality was this sexual aggression and the fact that her mother was a whore and her father a pimp. That's why she had to take something to walk the streets. She's a broken girl. She's like a baby. Every once in a while she meets a guy who promises to take care of her and to get her out of it. So she stops hitting the streets for a few months. She really tried to get herself out. Several times. But she was always treated badly by social workers. The ones she saw never knew how to listen to her and understand. So she continues, and it's been going on for seven years . . ."

Outside of the most dramatic cases, the majority of us have stayed in the *quartiers*. In one way or another, we wanted to help through our commitment to effect change. Some of us who became teachers immediately asked to be assigned to an at-risk school district [*zone d'éducation prioriataire*]. Others became activists in organizations, educators, or volunteer social workers [*femme relais*]. Many of us believe that nothing is inevitable; that's why we have to take care of the youngest, educate them, help them to succeed in school, and keep them from hanging out on the streets.

Do you think that women should play a role in the *quartiers*?

The responses to this question are mixed. However, a little more than half of us find it normal to invest ourselves in our neighborhood. It is more than just the place where we live. How? On which issues? What can we contribute? Among those who responded to this question, the two themes most often cited were the education of children and the bonds between generations.

We would also like to help our parents; that is normal, after all. So the little we earn at work goes to our parents. Within our family, in the *quartiers*, we are prepared to take care of everyone: parents, brothers and sisters, friends, the neighborhood; our condition as women, our education, everything pushes us toward altruism and solidarity. We are all proud of our loyalty. Mayors, school administrators, those in charge of the few public services that remain in our neighborhoods, they all know that without us things would be much worse.

But for all of that, are they ready to recognize our knowhow, our capacity for social mediation and conflict management? Are they truly trying to help us reduce the violence to which we fall victim? Do they view us as anything other than a conduit for their own policies? Of course not. For want of anything better, they pay homage to us. At conferences and in official speeches, they continually praise our work, our exemplary benevolence, our commitment to serving the collectivity. But for once, we are going to say it clearly: we are tired of homage. Ladies and gentlemen, we have no use for your recognition or your friendship. What we want is for you to take up your responsibilities when we assume ours.

Urban Violence

Violence is always a difficult topic to broach. First, of course, because it brings us back to our own story, to the most dramatic events of our lives, precisely the ones we would like to forget. But also because violence against women is still taboo, and the silence surrounding it largely contributes to the development of a strong sense of guilt among the victims, particularly because they are women, which in turn feeds the silence and the taboos. Doubtless this explains why the majority of responses to these questions on our questionnaires are negative.

Nevertheless, one thing is striking when we analyze the relationships between men and women in the *quartiers*. It is the violence, manifest and explicit, in all of its facets and all of its manifestations. The testimony that we were able to collect frequently mentions this problem. Regarding women, the first thing you think of is sexual violence in all its forms. For a long time, these attacks were absent from public discourse. One reason for this is that sexual violence is one of the principal domains of masculine domination. In a traditionally patriarchal society such as French society, sexual and sexist violence is denied. For the last few years, the media have focused attention on incest and pedophilia; more recently, the phenomenon of gang rape has become a subject of great interest. Certainly, that is a first step toward lifting the veil and overcoming taboos.

However, the manner in which these attacks are treated is not satisfactory. Take gang rape, for example. We all know that collective rapes exist in the *quartiers*. To what extent? Are they as widespread as certain news stories would lead us to believe? That is impossible to verify. We all know guys who are quick to brag about things they would not own up to so easily if they had really committed those acts. That said, journalists believe they have discovered something new in gang rape. In it, they see the sign of the supreme barbarity that prevails in neighborhoods ruined by urban crowding. What a surprise for them to find out a few weeks ago that an eleven-year-old girl living in a quiet part of a small, provincial town had been raped regularly by several young middle-school students for nearly a year! In reality, all the testimony shows that gang rapes are not limited to the ghettos and that these atrocious rapes are not on the rise.

He saw his sister, he opened fire on everyone, and he committed suicide
Marie-Claire, the principal of a junior high school

"A few years ago, two of our students died the same night, a brother and sister. The boy was fifteen years old, his sister thirteen. That evening, some friends came looking for him at his house. They had organized a gang rape in an abandoned shack not too far away. It was some guys from another neighborhood that he didn't know very well, but he followed them. When they got there, the rape had already begun. And it was his sister. So he lost it. He returned to his parents' place, he took his father's gun, he went back, and he opened fire on everyone, first his sister, then the others. Then he turned the gun on himself. At school we had to deal with it. Everyone was traumatized, including us. It was weeks before we got professional help to handle the situation."

On the matter of sexual violence, the data is scarce. The police statistics on rape reveal only part of the reality, because today, as in the past, the victims do not dare to press charges. In 2000, a national study on violence against women was conducted by the research team "Enveff" (*Populations et sociétés*, no. 364 [January 2001]). The merit of this study is that it addressed every aspect of violence that women can experience, both in public and elsewhere. Over the twelve months in which the research was conducted, 22 percent of women under the age of twenty-five were victims of sexual harassment (in the broad sense) in public. Whether it is a question of insults, threats, touching, exhibitionism, or more serious attacks, young women are the first victims of violence. That said, every age range was affected, even older women (from forty-five to fifty-nine years of age). More generally, the researchers estimate that fifty thousand women between the ages of twenty and fifty-nine are victims of rape every year in France.

We have no statistical data on adolescents or on what happens in schools. But a study conducted in 1996 by the National Agency on AIDS showed that 15.4 percent of girls under eighteen who are already sexually active have experienced an unwanted sexual encounter. Over the past few years, public debate has focused on pedophilia and incest. The reality and the magnitude of this kind of violence needed to be revealed; nevertheless, we must not obscure the fact that in the vast majority of cases, rapes of adolescents are perpetrated by boys in the same age range. In any case, this study reveals that rape is not particularly concentrated in one type of high school or another: there is no gap among general, technical, or professional high schools. Consequently, rape is not socially specific, and we must be wary of every temptation to stigmatize.

On the other hand, there are certain things we know about the sexual violence experienced by young girls: the perpetrators tend to be repeat offenders, and they have often been past victims themselves; and as for the victim, the act tends to be repeated. Much has been done to prevent pedophilia, but we have failed to produce campaigns and actions directed toward adolescents themselves. That certainly explains one part of the overall increase in sexist violence of all kinds: verbal insults, touching, jokes, and all sorts of comments have become common practice, particularly in schools. This can be seen across the board. There are other phenomena that are not found everywhere in the same way or to the same extent: in at-risk schools or in certain professional high schools, people on the ground have observed a climate of consistent aggressiveness among boys and girls: "small" acts of violence occur daily. There is no more real *mixité* between boys and girls, and their only interaction stems from power struggles.[2] We have to be worried as these behaviors become more radical.

2. On the notion of *mixité*, see fn. 5 in the Introduction.

Violence is not always physical. It also plays out significantly through words, tone, remarks, and jokes that are more or less sexist. If the Enveff study highlights the catastrophic situation in public spaces, it also addresses the multiple forms of domestic and workplace violence. There, as well, the results shed light on the difficulties that young women encounter. Overall, 15 to 20 percent of women had been victims of psychological pressure at work. Ten percent had been insulted or threatened over the past year, 5 percent had experienced emotional harassment, and 4 percent had been victims of sexual harassment. Within couples, 10 to 20 percent of women have experienced domestic violence. But psychological pressure and emotional blackmail are most widespread within families: 37 percent of the women questioned had been subjected to disparaging comments and remarks in 2000 (51 percent of women in the youngest age range)! The most common ground for violence against women remains behind the couple's closed doors.

Derogatory Comments

Nassera, a salaried employee

"I've always wanted my independence. What I couldn't stand anymore was the differential treatment of girls and boys. To not have the right to go out, to have boyfriends. Sexuality was totally taboo, the big Satan. In adolescence it's terrible. Some of my girlfriends felt like they weren't normal because they were beginning to wonder about their bodies, their impulses. Faced with that, my choice was rebellion. There, too, I was out of step because I was affirming an individual choice in a milieu where that isn't done, especially for a girl. Leaving was the only way to affirm this choice.

"When you're a girl living in a housing project, there are comments when you're waiting for the bus, derogatory comments. That's also why I wanted to leave. I couldn't stand it that guys allowed themselves to talk to me however they wanted. I reacted strongly to that. Even today, the people I'm close to don't understand my choices. I got married four years ago, and I still don't have a child. People wonder what I'm waiting for."

What is striking in these statistics is that women are not safe anywhere. Wherever they go, whatever their age, violence is an integral part of their daily lives. Everything happens as if brutality were "natural." Debates about security as they are currently formulated focus attention on delinquency or trafficking of all kinds. Far be it from us to contradict these observations. However, it must be recognized, one way or another, that violence against women is probably the most common and the most accepted form of violent crime. The great national debate on crime, invoked on all sides by candidates during the presidential elections, cannot take place without listening to our voices; otherwise, it will be pointless.

Sexuality: Zero Plus Zero Equals Zero

Sexuality in the questionnaires

If we believe the questionnaire responses, sexuality does not seem to be a problem. To the question of whether you feel power over your choices on the matter of sexuality, the majority responded yes. On the same note, the majority of us feel that we are able to make individual choices with complete freedom. Here there is a theme of real satisfaction. Nevertheless, we have to nuance these responses. First of all, because most of us are already activists, we have a different approach to sexuality than the majority of women in the *quartiers*. From this point of view, our responses are probably not representative of the reality. If we dig a little deeper, we realize that other responses contradict this optimism. So in terms of our demands for information, many of us make access to contraception as well as family and conjugal rights a top priority. As a result, things are more complicated than they might seem at first glance.

In the testimony that we were able to gather, in the discussions at the local Special Assemblies, sexuality showed up more often as a problem than as a form of individual choice exercised in complete freedom. Just as with violence, sexual taboos remain strong at the heart of the family and impose silence upon us more often than they grant liberty. The problems are particularly marked during adolescence, at the age when we discover our desires, when our bodies change—at the age when we ask ourselves questions that are more complex than children's dreams of princesses and superheroes.

It might go without saying, but it is probably better to say it: the school should be a site for education about sexuality. That should be the case for all young people, but it is crucial for the girls and boys from the housing projects, since in our families, sexuality is a subject that is obviously never talked about between parents and children. On another note, sexism, the absence of *mixité*, and in fact the actual segregation between girls and boys that has taken over in the *quartiers* can only increase the lack of sexual fulfillment and engender aggression, contempt, and repression at an age when sexuality is already so confusing.

We must say it directly: it's a wasteland out there. At school, these questions are not broached until middle school in the form of two hours of discussion a year in eighth and ninth grade. Sex education is included in the programs for AIDS prevention, but it is not a subject of discussion in and of itself. It is nevertheless a curious approach to sexual and emotional education for adolescents: the association of sex and love with illness creates a problem that is not inconsequential for the way that adolescents might come to see relationships between men and women.

Certainly the prevention of sexually transmitted diseases must remain a priority. During the last World AIDS Day (December 1, 2001), officials from the Ministry of National Education and Health organized a roundtable with students' parents and the organizations involved in the fight against STDs and with the emotional and sexual education of teens. The reports were devastating. The key actors all pointed to the slackening of prevention and to the increase in risky practices among young people. Many, particularly the boys, do not know how to use a condom or believe that you can reuse them . . . Others simply refuse to use them, saying they are not comfortable or that there has to be trust . . .

As for girls and contraception, the bottom line there is not good, either. Many adolescents from the *quartiers* have no idea how to obtain contraceptives. Many have never heard of family planning centers and do not dare consult the school nurses who could inform them. It must be said that there are not many nurses in the schools. So the rare days when they come onto school grounds are essentially devoted to treating minor injuries and illnesses and the flu. That makes it hard to go to the nurse for information in front of ten other students who have come to get a packet of aspirin. In short, there is still much to be done so that access to contraception will cease to be a problem for so many adolescents.

Before abortion was legalized

Sarah, a student

"I don't believe I've ever asked myself the question about abortion. I mean that I naïvely took it as a given. And then last year I read this book by Annie Ernaux called *The Event*. She tells how when she was a student like me, she got pregnant, just like that, by accident. She wanted an abortion. But at that time abortion wasn't legal. You had to find the money and pay a woman for a back-alley abortion. She recounts her journey, her doubts, the pain, the solitude. I believe it was then that I really became aware of what happened before. Now I understand the feminist movement better, and I feel closer to it."

Recently we saw ministers congratulating themselves on the current poster campaign about contraception being led by the Ministry of Employment and

Solidarity. Yet we've known for a long time that these campaigns are effective only if they are accompanied by a mobilization of the people involved, or by initiatives allowing young people and women to express themselves, to inform themselves, and to hold discussions. Thus once again it all comes down to the goodwill of a few people at the grassroots level. Even if teachers and nurses in some educational establishments mobilize themselves, those actions remain marginal and do not come anywhere close to reaching all the students.

Concerns about the lack of sexual fulfillment and access to contraception are not limited to adolescents. In our organizations, we regularly meet married women who have been raped by their husbands and endured unwanted pregnancies because they had no access to contraception, and no access to the right to abortion or to pleasure . . .

The organization is her only refuge
Maria, a community organizer in a Parisian banlieue

"There is a woman who regularly comes to the organization. She has lived in France for twenty-six years, and she hasn't seen her family since she got married. Her husband forbids her. She is like a prisoner. This woman experiences no pleasure in her lovemaking: no surprise there; her husband routinely rapes her. She is also beaten in front of her own children! She feels as though the children have more of a say than she does. She is not given any responsibility within her family. Of course, she strives to educate her children. But in that kind of climate, it's not easy. She has no access to money. She doesn't even have the means to buy herself feminine products. The last time she gave birth, they had to make her underwear to wear to the hospital. For her, divorce is unimaginable. If she left her husband, she would immediately be rejected by her family and her community. So she continues to hope that things will change. That the blows will stop. In reality, the organization is her only refuge; we are her second family."

Sexuality today is one of the areas in which the degradation of our condition as women shows itself most clearly. Wherever we turn, we search in vain for a reason to be optimistic: silence from government institutions on one side, which, as usual, depend entirely on nonprofit organizations; the degraded status of women on the other, which perpetuates itself because girls have no model besides their mothers, who are more used to kowtowing than to holding their heads high.

You Bitch! The Banality of Sexism

Last year, an ad for a brand of eyeglasses dared to show a myopic hunter gunning down his dog after mistaking it for a wild boar. Protests from the gun lobby, a thorough apology from the manufacturer, and the affair was over. The same year, a brand of cosmetics presented a list of beauty secrets. In the photo a woman looks at the magic booklet and says, "This year, I will read a book." Women are stupid and useless, isn't it a well-known fact? At dinner parties in the city, dumb blonde jokes seem very *à la mode*; but wait . . . we are reminded that these are only jokes. Everyone thinks it is normal for gun enthusiasts to protest the humor in ads. But whenever women object to sexist jokes and the banality of machismo, the response is about freedom of expression and artistic creation, or it's accusations of conscience policing and bitterness. It is as if sexism were part of the cultural patrimony of the average Joe, as if feminists were nothing but a band of hysterics—as suffragettes were accused of being in their time, just for demanding the right to vote. In order to be heard, we now have to defend ourselves for being feminists. Or maybe we should just act like those oafs who, before hurling the most vile insults, begin by announcing, "I'm not racist, but . . ."

Can we laugh about everything, can we laugh at ourselves?
Sandra, a feminist activist

"My commitment as a feminist has grown stronger and stronger over the years. And I am becoming more and more aggressive about ads and sketches that ridicule women. I don't think we can laugh about everything. Jamel has a sketch about rape.[3] Okay, fine, he makes fun of everything. But at the same time, he always presents himself as a young guy from the *quartiers*. And precisely because he comes from there, I find it disgusting, because that really exists, and I'm not at all sure that it's funny for the girls who are victims; and moreover, that trivializes the act. It's less dramatic because we can laugh at it."

We are not naïve. It is important to be able to laugh at others and ourselves. Our problem is that nowadays sexism takes up all the space. We look in vain for ads in which we are valorized through something other than household products or the education of children. And all this time, the pornography industry is making millions selling women's bodies. On the boulevards of

3. Jamel Debbouze is a successful actor, comedian, and producer of Moroccan descent. —Trans.

big cities, thousands of women, minors, "imported" from the East or from Africa, are displayed on the pavement like merchandise. Everything is for sale, especially when you are a woman.

Prostitution and Feminism

Séverine, a teacher and activist

"With young people, especially boys, we've been working on respect for women for a while. We try to convey the idea that they must change their behavior, be less aggressive, respect the other person's wishes. But sometimes I think there's no point in it, because in my neighborhood there's no small amount of prostitution. It's dramatic because it's often very young girls, minors who come from the East. Obviously I don't condemn the girls. Obviously they are not there by choice, and they are caught up in networks of slavery that exploit them scandalously. But that's really difficult to explain to young boys, and even to the girls. It blurs the lines for them when it comes to emotional and sexual relationships. Adolescents end up thinking that sex is neutral and that it has no consequences. And that's without even taking account of the fact that all these adolescents have easy access to pornography. Except that nothing they do is ever discussed, and they don't talk about it at school or at home."

Nonetheless, there is still room for debate between prohibition and indifference. Room for public opinion campaigns (conducted with a selective filter, of course), room for cracking down on slavery and pimping, room for social action on behalf of the victims.

Men as objects, women as objects: the commodification of the body

Véronique

"Frankly, ads with shirtless men don't bother me. First of all, some of them are very attractive, and *we* need to see beautiful images, too, after all. And besides, for once it's not women who are considered objects . . . that's a change!"

Djalila

"Yes, okay, for aesthetics. But it all depends on how we treat nudity. There are some photos that are really beautiful and others that aren't. In the ads, for example, that use a shirtless man to sell beef, I don't see how that's going to move things forward. It's degrading for the guy, and on top of that, it changes our relationship to the body; the body becomes one commodity among others. That's what's shocking."

Everything Is Changing and Nothing Changes: Professional Training and Access to Employment

Girls, as everyone knows, do better in school than boys. From the perspective of exam success rates, the statistics are unambiguous. For example, although 76 percent of male candidates passed their baccalaureate in June 2001, 81 percent of the female candidates successfully passed this test. Whether it is the professional school certificate (BEP/CAP), the baccalaureate, or a university diploma, the results all attest to the spectacular silent revolution that has occurred in national education over the past thirty years: the popularization of access to secondary and then university education would not have happened without girls. Nowadays, 55 percent of students are women. Moreover, their academic trajectory is less erratic than that of boys: they repeat grades less often, they are less likely to drop out before receiving their diplomas, and so on. The girls of the *quartiers* have largely benefited from this general movement, which has touched all social classes. In the past fifteen years, the number of girls who leave high school without a diploma has been reduced to a third of what it was, and more of them have gone on to higher education. In short, the outcome for girls with respect to access to education and to diplomas is one of the rare areas where we can see a measurable improvement in our condition.

We might have expected that this tremendous increase in the level of achievement of girls from the *quartiers* would translate into concrete changes in access to employment, professional equality, or recognition of their abilities. But old habits die hard: everything has changed in schools, but nothing has changed in the workforce.

Despite soothing discourses about the return of growth and the creation of jobs, the situation for women from the *quartiers* who are looking for jobs has not really improved in the last fifteen years. From many perspectives, it has even gotten worse. Unemployment, lousy jobs, and money problems have become our daily bread; part-time work is our lot even when we want to work full-time; many of us are hired for low-level jobs that have nothing to do with our abilities and our degrees. And as if that were not enough, we have to add racial discrimination to all these other forms of inequality. For girls named Dalila or Malika who are enrolled in a professional training program, finding internships is not easy. During the hiring process, it is even more apparent. We all know girls who have been turned down for a job "because you must understand, Miss, the clients don't like people like you." Discrimination is everywhere; it is a huge problem, and it is a daily occurrence. It is impossible to say what happened to the growth that was supposed to resolve all the problems. Maybe it got lost along the way; in any case, it did not reach us.

I think it's because my name is Dalila
Soraya, a community organizer

"A few days ago, I met with a student who was seventeen years old. She was in her third year at a professional school, and she needed to do an internship at a company in the field she was interested in. It happened to be computer science. For weeks she made calls and sent letters. A friend even helped her write a résumé. She received only negative responses. First I asked her whether any of her teachers had given her a list of companies to contact, but apparently she had nothing. Then I asked her what hadn't gone well when she was looking for internships. She concluded that it's because her name is Dalila and she's Arab. It's lamentable that she's only a teen, and already she has internalized the idea that she will be a victim of discrimination all her life."

In France, there are laws in place that make this kind of professional inequality and discrimination illegal. Why are we waiting to apply them? Do we have the means? There are even fewer workforce inspectors in this country than there are school nurses; you get the point . . .

Communitarianism and the Weight of Tradition

In France, it is not easy to raise questions about religion and the weight of tradition. Conflicts between the republican state and religious institutions punctuate the history of the twentieth century. French secularism [*laïcité*] has always rested on a compromise between the political authorities and the clergy, which has limited each side to strictly defined roles: discourse on the family and morality goes to religious leaders, management of public affairs goes to politicians. In the sixties and seventies, feminists brought patriarchal oppression to light, but the struggle was essentially concerned with control over women's bodies and equal rights. The feminist movement never really succeeded in changing the game with family behaviors, as the studies on the division of household chores and domestic violence attest. With respect to the *quartiers*, a certain discourse promoted by a few intellectuals ended up being imposed: in the name of respecting cultural differences, we have to guard against denouncing traditions even if they are brutal and mutilating for women.

We must make ourselves understood on this point. We are in no way interested in questioning all traditions or all religious practices. Tradition and rituals are not the essential cause of our oppression. Only some practices need to be denounced and suppressed. Excision, polygamy, and forced marriages continue to exist. The mutilation of women's bodies, the lack of recognition of their status outside of marriage, are always the prelude to a poor self-image, and often lead to sexual misery and emotional catastrophe.

Forced marriage happens every day. In many Arab-Muslim families, girls are raised with this end in mind. From a very young age, they are taught to serve their father and brothers, and to be quiet. They eventually convince themselves that they will attain a full and complete existence only when they are married. When they reach a certain age, their parents and those around them pressure the young girls until they finally give in. Sometimes things happen suddenly: the family is on vacation abroad, and a man is presented to the young girl, who cannot refuse because her father holds her passport. Sometimes the girl is not even present when the marriage ceremony takes place. As far as people are concerned, everyone is fine with picking a husband for her. There are also times when these things happen in France.

Marrying So As Not to Be the Shame of the Family

Sonia talks about the forced marriage of one of her friends

"We've known each other forever; we grew up together. She went out a lot; she had a certain freedom. But her parents saw her as a wayward daughter. And there's the pressure of people around them, who make remarks. So one day her father went to see her mother. He told her that her daughter was the shame of the family. The mother cried, of course, and that's where the pressure began; her mother, her brothers, she had everyone on her back. In the space of one day, everything changed. She no longer had the right to do anything. That lasted for months, months of conflict, months of remarks about everything and nothing. At a certain point, she ended up cracking. She agreed to meet potential suitors. One, then another, then a third, and so on, until finally her mother told her to stop. For lack of a better option, she ended up choosing the fifth one because he was the youngest and a little more open than the rest. They dated a little, not for very long, and then after a month, the parents organized a traditional marriage. From that day on, the criticism and the conflict began. They had a child, and then it got worse. She was beaten. Her parents, of course,

> knew about it. They felt guilty. The guy was a bad husband. That's why they eventually accepted divorce. But at that moment, it wasn't a dishonor anymore, because it was the guy's fault, and my friend had married traditionally. I think that says a lot about the hypocrisy of families."

Psychological pressure plays a central role. Young girls want to resist, refuse, say no. But standing your ground for months is extremely difficult, and because dishonor must be avoided at all cost, girls end up giving in for the sake of their families. Often things are even more insidious. It is not unusual for women to choose marriage by default, even though they are not really in love. In those cases, the parents do not technically organize things. That said, the weight of their upbringing is such that women feel uncomfortable when they see their sisters and friends getting married one after the other. On the other hand, they all know that marriage is not only their destiny but, above everything else, their parents' profound wish. Guilt is added to the lack of options; they believe they must become a woman through marriage and "choose" whoever seems like he would be best at fulfilling his duties as a husband. That can work; but in several cases we know of, this supposed choice has been the prelude to emotional catastrophe. Formally, they were not coerced. Nobody dragged them by force to the ceremony. But for all that, is it a genuine choice?

Patriarchy is a system of family organization that is perpetuated by raising young women to be submissive, as well as through direct control over marriage. You have to choose a man from the community, preferably from a family your family knows, coming from the same region as your family or even from the same country. In this way, it is guaranteed that "tradition" will be transmitted to the next generation. Mixed marriages are not looked upon favorably, and freely chosen unions even less so. That is why the practice of arranged marriage is still going on in 2002. That said, many women refuse these marriages. Mixed marriages exist in spite of everything. Some couples choose not to marry. But then they have to struggle. Prejudices have a long life within and beyond the family. The psychological pressure is real for those who take the path to emancipation. They say so themselves; they had to engage in a true struggle.

It's a Struggle We Took On Together

> **Safia, a community organizer**
>
> "I was a student in Lyons. I had an apartment. I had been going out with my boyfriend for four years, and he moved to be with me. My family is Muslim, and leaving home to live with your boyfriend just isn't done; it shames the family.

But I broke the taboos, and I told my parents that he was coming to live with me. But I should say that I have a unique personality. I've always been a bit like that . . . My parents were used to it. They weren't really okay with it, but they accepted it all the same. His side was another thing. They're very religious, and I was viewed as the girl who had kidnapped their son. But they still wanted to meet me. Obviously, their objective was for us to marry. We could have done it, of course, for others, for the community. We knew it would make our parents happy and it would stop people from talking. But I thought I was too young, and I didn't know whether he was the man of my life. In the end, today they are proud. Our two families accepted our choice. They have even come to our defense in front of those who make comments. I was presented to my in-laws back in his village; we were able to share the same bedroom. But we had to get people to accept all of that. We both did a lot of talking, him with his parents and me with my brothers, and everyone understood. We're happy like this, and it has lasted thirteen years. I have the same obligations as a married woman, but not completely. I don't belong to him, I don't use his name, and I feel free vis-à-vis my community. Of all the girls I know, I must be the only one who is living with someone. My friends tell me that I'm lucky to have such an open-minded family. Maybe so, but we took on the struggle, and we took it on together."

More than a few people are worried by these girls' rebellion. Many men and fathers would like to be able to avoid these situations that cast opprobrium on the family. No doubt this explains why a number of boys in the past few years have gone back to their country of origin looking for a spouse. For them, a submissive and docile woman raised with a strict respect for tradition seems easier to find there. Patriarchy definitely still knows how to find a way to reproduce itself . . . It also rests on direct social control exercised by the community. In the *quartiers*, the neighbors assume for themselves the right to monitor young girls' and even married women's lives. Rumor plays a major role. The surveillance of women is constant, inside and outside the family.

Many women have to lie in order to manage the few liberties they have. You can go out, but secretly. You can have a boyfriend, but nobody can know about it. It is not surprising, then, that under these conditions some adolescents choose to take refuge in a kind of pseudo-liberty outside this communal straitjacket: officially submissive, they reject all constraints and all limits when they are outside their communities. But of course, this total reversal is rarely a real choice. Having learned from a young age to distrust boys and to view sex with disgust, they know nothing of pleasure, and they ignore their desires.

Fleeing, then, is no more liberating than submitting. In many ways, the two are alike.

However, there has to be a middle ground between docility and self-destruction. There does not necessarily have to be a contradiction between religious practice and the affirmation of one's identity as a woman. We think it is possible for respect for one's origins and for freedom of choice to coexist harmoniously. To achieve this balance, we have to make an effort to transmit family histories, and especially those of immigrant families, to men and women of the *quartiers*. Today this knowledge is lacking. Why and how did the first generations come to France? How did the adults experience the wars of independence, police repression in France, racism in the factories, the misery of shantytowns? This type of memory exists only in an embryonic state where certain activists have been able to lead the effort. In its absence, traditions and values are transmitted only through the authority of masculine domination. Women are forced to accept it; they are not able to sort out what is fair from what is not, to separate out the rituals that threaten their liberties from those that can be respected. Not all traditions are abhorrent. It is patriarchy and control by the community that oppress us, nothing more, nothing less.

I Hold On to My Double Culture
Nadia, a nonprofit activist

"In my family, during my turbulent adolescence, I was regarded as a kneejerk rebel, someone who opposed every form of dogmatism in my parents' teaching out of a pure love of contradiction. I wouldn't accept the idea that just because my name was Nadia and I was of Moroccan descent that I had to have an education tailored to order, conforming to a certain set of rites and traditions. From a young age, I categorically refused to be recognized only through my belonging to a group; I wanted to be recognized for my individuality. I say that in hindsight: ten years separate me from that girl who rebelled, mainly alone, because nobody was capable of understanding everything that oppressed her. At the age of fifteen or sixteen, when you hit puberty, that's when, in Muslim families, you really notice that the life the religious community has in mind for you includes far more constraints than it does for boys. So at this age I was opposed to being treated differently on the pretext that I was a girl, particularly where marriage was concerned. For example, in front of my family I proudly maintained that I would marry whomever I wanted and that I didn't give a damn about what the community expected. I thought that the choice was mine, end of story! Today I love a man who is nothing like what my cultural background would predestine. But I changed. I grew up, and my relationship to the world also changed. I abandoned the strategy of opposing dogma impulsively; I sidestep it, I work on it, and I'm convinced that things will improve through dialogue and discussion. My emancipation happened through my upbringing, through dialogue with my parents. It's true that I'm lucky to have parents who, despite the weight of tradition and religion, knew how to prove to me that they were progressive in their own way. A confrontation would have led only to a rupture with my family, and I'm incapable of living with that fracture. I hold on to my double culture, and I refuse to sacrifice one in favor of the other; both are foundational to my personality and make me who I am. After all, everyone has their own contradictions; it's enough to know how to articulate them, to integrate them into everyday life."

When family and collective memory is hidden, this can also create favorable conditions for the development of much more serious tendencies. Extremist groups rely on this ignorance to extend their influence in the *quartiers*. The implantation process is well known. Fascist organizations and cults have used it in their own times. In the beginning, an organization proposes activities that seem harmless: help with work, cultural activities, language classes, religious education, help networks. Considering the resources at these organizations' disposal, and the social situation in the *quartiers*, it obviously works. But under the cover of these organizations, little by little militants are recruited who eventually swell the ranks of *intégrisme*.[4] They are inculcated with religious precepts that have nothing to do with the tolerant Islam practiced by the great majority of Muslims in France. It is that much easier when boys are ignorant of their heritage and their traditions. We need not go into detail; this radical extremism treats women with extreme brutality.

We must say it straightforwardly: this *intégrisme* is a form of fascism. If it walks like fascism and talks like fascism and is violent, then . . . The activists who struggle against these organizations know it well; all of them have paid the price and have suffered fatwas, insults, and threats. We must not let

4. While it is tempting to translate *intégriste* or *Islam intégriste* as "radical," "extremist," or "fundamentalist" Islam, that is not exactly correct. To be sure, *intégriste* religious movements (in all monotheistic faiths, including Islam, Christianity, and Judaism) are often extremist and fundamentalist in nature, but *intégrisme* refers specifically to the desire for a political system whose laws are subordinate to or integrated with religious decree and doctrine. In general, these movements do not approve of the separation of church and state. They advocate and work toward a single state religion to the exclusion of other faiths and even other forms of religious practice within the given faith. —Trans.

down our guard in a single case. *Intégrisme* is a vile beast that threatens our neighborhoods.[5]

Silence Is Our Enemy

The scene we have just broadly sketched might seem dark. In many ways it is, because it attests to a real deterioration of our condition. Who could have predicted just fifteen years ago that things would fall apart so quickly when during the sixties, seventies, and early eighties women saw continual progress in their status, their rights, and their liberties in French society? Who can understand this situation today with respect to girls' academic success, to the increase in women working? Who can accept this waste of human beings? There is a major social contradiction that we have to try to explain if we want to pull ourselves out of this situation.

Silence seems to be the first cause of this collapse. It is first of all our silence. We all know that isolation is the principal source of our oppression. To face the psychological pressure from the family or community alone, to brave the danger of public places alone, to fight individually against ignorance and prejudice: all of that is nearly impossible, and nobody is expected to do the impossible. Year after year, we joined nonprofit organizations, unions, and sometimes even political parties in large numbers, convinced that things would not change magically, which is true, but that they could evolve provided that we fought for change. Today we have to admit that this is not enough. Our struggle until now has been limited partly by the absence of an organized and identifiable feminist movement in the *quartiers*. For that reason, women's speech, when it exists, remains too often confined to organization meetings, and it does not exist as a recognized and legitimate perspective in public and political space.

In our neighborhoods, the feminist movement has experienced two fundamental setbacks whose consequences still are not fully understood. First, feminism has largely been discredited, in the *quartiers* more than elsewhere. To affirm oneself openly as a feminist is enough to be accused of being bitter or hysterical, at least when we are not being told that we simply need to get laid. Even worse, our struggle provokes smirks and irony: "Those women, now what do they want?" Sometimes our own girlfriends, seeking peace through anonymity and discretion, react negatively when we come to the defense of a woman or when we condemn the return of machismo.

5. "Vile beast" is a translation of the French *la bête immonde*, and comes from a line in Bertolt Brecht's play *The Resistible Rise of Arturo Ui*. The phrase is generally used as a synonym for fascism. —Trans.

Me, a Feminist? Certainly Not!

Myriam, a student

"In the beginning, for me, feminism was a struggle for hysterical and bitter women. Moreover, I found it useless. At the time, I thought that if we could solve the social issues, it would also solve women's problems at the same time. So there was no point; it would do much more good to struggle for the advancement of everybody's rights. Little by little, I changed. Through discussions with other girls, and especially with feminists, I understood that the question of women was an entirely different question. Today I not only call myself a feminist, but I also think that it is through this movement that we can learn to solve social problems."

This is certainly the second-greatest difficulty facing women's struggle; one is not born, but rather becomes, a feminist. Every activist for women's causes knows it: consciousness of oppression and knowledge of the history of former struggles are a necessary precondition for a feminist movement in the *quartiers*. These reference points are lacking. The current generation of girls knows nothing or very little about women's condition before the legalization of access to contraception or abortion; nothing about the fight for the right to vote, which after all was not so long ago; nothing about the difficulties that our mothers encountered in trying to get their families to accept the idea of divorce or the freedom to work. Just as they are ignorant of their own families' histories of immigration, they totally ignore this other story, the one of women's struggle. It has to be said that we frankly are not getting any help from the institutions that have brought our situation to an impasse.

Radio Silence: Institutional Action on the Condition of Women

Whether it is a question of violence, sexuality, education, or even of work again, we are struck by the deafening degree of institutional silence. That is in no way meant to imply that at the grassroots level, actors, activists, and government employees are unaware of the difficulty of being a woman or the need to denounce violence, discrimination, or economic uncertainty. But with the way that institutions currently function, these debates are never faced head on. It is as if institutions have to make excuses for addressing the condition of women by burying such issues within greater social problems, even if it means ignoring a large part of these problems.

Sometimes, of course, institutions develop discourses that denounce practices such as sexual violence in schools or racial discrimination in hiring practices. However, until the appropriate structures and measures are put in place, these edifying words are like incantations and have no concrete consequences. This is especially true with respect to women's vulnerability in the workforce. It has been more than twenty years since the laws on professional equality between men and women were passed, laws based on universally recognized facts and extremely thorough research. However, despite the speeches, the circulars, the conventions, and the laws, there are no real permanent mechanisms to punish unequal treatment. For us, there is still a huge difference between formal rights and real rights.

Local Initiatives

In spite of everything, there are local initiatives just about everywhere in France. Over the past year, the work of dozens of local assemblies within the network of the National Federation has provided us with a preliminary overview of these initiatives. Locally, organizations were able to initiate activities that provided occasions for women to find a voice. Everywhere, circles for women interested in sewing, world cuisine, or literacy have been developed in the *quartiers*. These organizations put on any number of festivities—multicultural parades, concerts, block parties—all of which are occasions for creating bonds of solidarity.

The Sewing Circle: A Network for Solidarity

Celine, a community organizer in a Parisian banlieue

"A few years ago, we created a sewing group that welcomed all the women from the neighborhood who wanted to participate. The goal is to make traditional clothing or other garments yourself. It's important in itself because these women, who often have no access to money and have difficulty buying clothes, take a certain amount of pride in producing something useful and beautiful. We take photos of these garments, and it's always an occasion for a party. They put their entire hearts into it. But it goes much farther than that. Because while sewing, we discuss their stories and their situations with them; we try to help them in tangible ways, but also to encourage them to become aware that their situation isn't unchangeable, whatever it is. It's a real network of solidarity."

The point of these actions is not to take care of women who have been rendered helpless or broken down by social or marital problems. During the local assemblies, this issue was discussed at length. These activities are the "pedagogical foundation" for the development of women's voices. Thanks to this foundation, a history and a memory are transmitted. Alongside or parallel to these concrete actions, we have seen discussion groups and women's commissions emerge. Within our network, these places of exchange exist just about everywhere; they developed at the impetus of the local assemblies. It is a first step that we now have to prolong and extend, because it allows women to emerge from their isolation and become aware of their condition.

Overwhelming praise of organizations

Several questions pertained to assistance centers in the *quartiers*.[6] We asked about the places one might go in case of a problem and about the nature of the aid offered in these centers, for example. The responses were unambiguous: in the vast majority of cases, the responses overwhelmingly praised the actions of organizations that respond concretely to needs. They are a true resource in the event of difficulties, and they are also places where one is welcomed and listened to.

Large-Scale Self-Defense?

Despite the development of such initiatives, they remain marginal in comparison to the number of women who live in and enliven the *quartiers*. Our reactions to machismo and patriarchy, to discrimination and violence, are highly diverse. That said, they can all be traced back to the same logic, that of negating our individuality and our own identity. Sometimes our refusal of destiny has led us to flee from or to break with our families; the lack of a better option often leads us to submission, but we have also seen violent or hyper-individualist behaviors develop over the past few years, which are a sign that the ghetto has also gained ground in our minds.

6. The term here is *lieux d'acceuil*. In French this can to refer to a welcome center for tourists, but it is also a common term for the generally nonprofit institutions that serve various community needs, from assisting cancer patients and their families, to helping new immigrants, to providing crisis centers for women who have been raped or abused. —Trans.

Breaking away to make my own choices
Malika, a journalist

"At the age of eighteen, I left home, the housing project where my parents live. It was a challenge for me; I wanted to make it in spite of all the difficulties. I broke away from my family and the neighborhood so that I could make my own choices and succeed at what I had always wanted to do—become a journalist. But I paid a price for it: I had to work to pay for my studies myself."

Adolescents are increasingly asking to be protected from violence, especially at school, but nothing has been done either collectively or institutionally. Each girl tends to come up with her own system of protection. In order to be left alone, some girls resort to imitating macho, masculine behavior: a good offense is the best defense. And alone is exactly what they get: in the projects, they are utterly alone. Girls who are aggressive toward boys, even physically attacking them, obviously do not do it for pleasure. Rather than avoid confrontation, they provoke it. They thereby earn respect. The problem is that winning a little peace in this way comes at a cost, a very high cost. First of all, they add to the aggressive and violent climate among adolescents. This kind of behavior also runs counter to any kind of *mixité* among boys and girls. Finally, for these girls, violence ends up becoming a normal mode of expression that they use not only against boys, but also against anyone who might pose a threat—adults, youth organizers, teachers, and so on. The phenomenon of hyper-violent gangs has largely developed over the past few years, even if such behaviors were already in existence.

The need for self-protection can also take much less visible but equally insidious forms. Some girls, when choosing their career path near the end of high school, head straight for traditionally female courses of study even though the professional opportunities are very limited. They know to expect temp work and unemployment down the road, but in the meantime they will be hassled less. They are often encouraged by parents who are perplexed and legitimately concerned about boy-girl interactions within more masculine fields. This is the only explanation for the concentration of girls in certain service industries: of course, familial and academic socialization of girls during early childhood, emphasizing altruism, self-sacrifice, and discretion, leaves its mark in combination with social representations of certain "feminine" careers (nursing, social work, youth organizing, teaching, working as a personal assistant, etc.). But we cannot blame everything on early childhood. For years now we have been driving home the point that employment opportunities in certain sectors are bad, that you cannot find a job with a secretarial degree, but that there are shortages in other sectors, notably in the industrial sectors. So not only is there a problem of information, but schools must be made to face their responsibilities, particularly when they are incapable of guaranteeing safety for adolescents on school grounds.

Another solution in the attempt to escape this climate is to conform to a stereotype. It is interesting, in this regard, to observe the behavior of girls at school, especially those who have chosen "atypical" career paths. The girls who pursue a typically male-oriented course of study are a priori more respected by their peers; it is as if their having asserted themselves by making a masculine choice no longer makes them "easy prey" for boys. In other words, to get a little peace, you have to renounce a certain femininity.

Even more interesting is what can be observed in courses of study that attract boys and girls equally, courses in physical education at universities or computer science. The girls seem to have to confine themselves to two stereotypes: the basketball player or the dancer. In the one case, they get respect by developing a physical and verbal aggressiveness close to the masculine type. Having the right "look" goes a long way: every feminine attribute and charm is banished. The aggression is real, and it is directed not only at other girls but also at instructors and adults in general. You have to constantly be tested and prove that you are ready for a confrontation. As for the "dancers," they seek refuge in another caricature. If they assert themselves as girls, particularly through their "look," they also seek protection in the group and in discretion. They do not makes waves or stand out. In contrast to the others, they are constantly harassed, groped, and subjected to jeering nicknames and double-edged gestures with sexual overtones. But they are victims collectively and not individually. In this case protection comes from negating self-assertion, whereas in the other case protection comes from denying one's gender identity.

With respect to identity, the situation for girls is very difficult. The search for protection and a defense against boys' behavior constrains them, no matter what they choose, to hide their individuality and confine themselves to a stereotype. It is even more difficult because girls do not support each other as a group. Quite the contrary. When masculine domination is accepted or reversed through aggression, individuality is doubly denied by those who discredit feminism. Neighborhood rumors are meant to maintain the bad reputations of those who have rebelled. Shame on them, and on those who wanted to follow in their footsteps. In order to exist, there seems to be only one solution: accept the models imposed by patriarchy.

The real danger in all of this is that *mixité* is being reconsidered, especially in schools. The logic of separation is beginning to prevail in some countries, including the United States and Australia. It is encouraged not only by conservative currents but, paradoxically, also by certain feminists, who, having noticed the deterioration of girls' situation, prefer to construct single-sex establishments to protect adolescents. In France, no matter what the authorities say, *mixité* is already being reconsidered. Two examples among others: in some middle schools, albeit only a small number, gym classes have become an occasion for separating boys and girls. In public spaces the logic of separation prevails as well, and even more clearly than in schools.

Reacting

This Special Assembly is a powerful moment for us, the women of the *quartiers*. Through workshops, we can share our experiences and reflect together to better understand oppression and find ways out from under masculine domination. This national meeting is a first step. It is the culmination of several months of work that came to fruition during the local assemblies. But we do not want to stay here, simply mapping out our ideas. If we are going to change our condition, we need to mobilize and get moving on all fronts: safety, professional inequality, discrimination, contesting patriarchy and communitarianism. Our words must be heard by all women, in the *quartiers* and beyond. We want to create a veritable feminist movement in the *quartiers*. For that, we can already count on the activist and organizational networks that have emerged in the past few years. Our cause is that of all women who want change and who struggle every day. We must nevertheless work with all women in order to move consciousness forward. We must formulate claims. We must appeal to elected officials, unions, CEOs. The road will be long and difficult. We are ready to take up these challenges. We must be reckoned with.

I want to run, but then what?
Morgiane, an activist and a municipal official

"It's difficult for a woman like me to convince people that I can run for political office. Everyone's fine with me hanging up posters or distributing flyers. But when it comes to running, that's another story. I have every kind of handicap. I am a woman, a child of immigrants, from the *quartiers*, and I'm an activist for a minority cause. I entered the race to be the party's candidate in the local elections in the northern neighborhoods of my city. The local administration of my party took an attitude toward me that was more than cautious. It was pretty difficult. A female candidate of Arab descent—that was a first in this city. They set up impediments for young people of immigrant descent who came out to vote. They asked them to bring proof of their voter registration, as if they were asking that of the other party members. There were schemes and insults; I was even personally threatened. That was a very difficult experience for me."

Winning the fight for political representation of young people in the *quartiers*

Samia, an antiracist activist

"I have been a member of this party for fifteen years. I believed that I was part of a progressive party, and then I discovered racism, and social contempt for the working class. In hindsight, I am now convinced that we cannot achieve victory without fighting for it. To get anything, you have to take it, and that is really hard. The young people who were with me felt humiliated and disappointed by all of that. Some even stopped working as activists completely. I believe that we must win the fight for the representation of young people from the *quartiers* in politics; without that, everything that is said about democratic integration means nothing, because when it's a question of power . . ."

The Manifesto of the Women of the *Quartiers*

Wherever men suffer, women bear this suffering. Economic marginalization and discrimination have built ghettos where men no longer see themselves as citizens equal to all others, and for women it is even worse. We are the women of these *quartiers* who have decided that we will no longer be silent in the face of the injustices we experience, and who refuse to be left to suffer in the name of "tradition," "religion," or simply violence.

Life in the *quartiers*, for the families who live there, for the children and their future, will not change unless we women regain our place and our dignity. We denounce the omnipresent sexism, the verbal and physical violence, the control of our sexuality, the gang rapes, the forced marriages, the brothers who set themselves up as guardians of the family honor or of the reputation of the housing project and who end up in prison. In denouncing all this, we reject the logic of the ghetto, which will imprison us permanently in its spiral if we do not revolt.

At a time when everyone is looking for an answer to the violence that undermines our society, we say that the first step must be our liberation and respect for our most basic rights. Public authorities, the media, and political parties see and speak only about the men of the *banlieues*. We appear only occasionally, as good girls, succeeding at school, or shown in the kitchen preparing the meal for a neighborhood festival.

Silence cloaks our lives. Silence about those who have run away, those who do housework from morning till night, those who have to hide their relationships, those who find themselves as mothers when they are hardly out of childhood themselves. We have decided not to wait until things go from bad to worse. We have decided to act in order to change our own lives, those of our families, and of our *quartiers*.

We are breaking taboos and speaking about things that usually remain hidden from others, and some will find this difficult to accept. To them we say: how will you overcome injustice, racism, exclusion, failure in school, prison, if you are our oppressors, you along with everyone else? Millions of women in the housing projects reject this false choice between submitting to the chaos of the ghetto or selling their bodies on the altar of survival.

Neither whores nor submissive. We are simply women who want the freedom to realize our desire for justice.

In pursuit of a voluntarist state policy that reinforces the values of the Republic and promotes social peace, we call for:[1]

The creation of structures that ensure access to basic rights:

The right to sex education for all, including:

- Information on the body
- Information on different forms of contraception
- Information on sexually transmitted diseases

The right to civic education, including:

- Advanced language instruction
- Courses in civic education
- Legal aid services supervised by professionals
- Knowledge of civil rights
- Access to information, guidance, and practical assistance if necessary

The right to safety and security for all:

- Services for victims of sexual harassment

The creation of emergency shelters for victims of:

- Psychological and physical violence (including domestic violence)
- Forced marriage and polygamy

The creation of reception services in police stations in connection with the offices pertaining to aid to women

The creation of legal measures allowing French consular services abroad to protect and repatriate women who are French citizens or foreigners living in France who have been forced into marriage

To fight against all the sources that channel women toward prostitution (polygamy, prostitution rings, being cut off from family)

In pursuit of the recognition of local associations, especially women's associations in the quartiers, as full actors in local and participatory democracy, we call for:

Significant and specific appropriations for the activities and the training of women in leadership positions in local organizations

Provision of locations and rooms to facilitate practices leading to greater engagement in democracy at the local level

1. A voluntarist state policy is one that relies on the voluntary action of citizens, nongovernmental organizations, and other institutions to realize policy goals. —Trans.

In pursuit of an urban policy that promotes mixité, we call for:

The creation of mixed programs

Promotion of actions aimed at better access to culture and leisure pursuits

Better recognition and representation of women's associations from the *quartiers* in state and regional measures

Promotion of any initiative creating links between city centers and the *quartiers*

In pursuit of a family policy that reduces the everyday burdens of women, we call for:

The establishment of new day-care centers

Measures that reduce the cost of day care

Measures that improve and support drop-in child care

In pursuit of a voluntarist employment policy, we call for:

Promotion of policies that support job security

Support for existing measures and systematic application of the law against all forms of discrimination in employment

Real, concrete application of the law protecting professional equality

In pursuit of a mixed-sex and democratic educational policy, we call for:

Maintaining and reinforcing the French melting pot, and promoting coeducation in all scholarly establishments

Improved career counseling services

Making career paths formerly reserved for boys more attractive and accessible to girls

Fighting against dead-end career paths that lead only to unskilled work or to unemployment

Introducing courses, from elementary through high school, that treat sex education, civic education, the equality of the sexes, and rights specific to girls

The Petition

Ni Putes Ni Soumises!

We, the women of the *quartiers*, living in housing projects on the outskirts of the city, with different origins, believers and nonbelievers, issue this appeal for our rights to freedom and emancipation.

Socially oppressed by a society that confines us in ghettos, which increase our poverty and exclusion. Smothered by the sexism of the men of our neighborhoods, who deny our basic rights in the name of "tradition."

We hereby unite for the first "Special Assembly of Women of the *Quartiers*," affirming our will to reclaim our rights, our freedom, our femininity. We refuse to be constrained by a false choice either to be submissive to the shackles of tradition or to sell our bodies in a consumer society.

- No more moral preaching. Our condition has deteriorated. The media and politicians have done little or nothing for us.
- No more victimization. We are fed up with others speaking for us and treating us with scorn.
- No more justifications of our oppression in the name of the right to difference and of respect for those who make us bow our heads.
- No more silence during public debates over violence, poverty, and discrimination.

The feminist movement has deserted the *quartiers*. The situation is urgent, and we have decided to act.

For us, the struggle against racism and exclusion and the struggle for our freedom and emancipation are one and the same. No one but we ourselves will liberate us from this double oppression.

We are speaking out and launching this appeal so that in each housing project in France, our sisters and our mothers will hear this cry for freedom and join our struggle for a better life in our neighborhoods.

Help us be heard. Distribute our call as widely as possible, and take part in the feminist and antiracist initiatives that are at the heart of our struggle!

Part II

Taking a Stand

Selections from *Scum of the Republic*
by Fadela Amara and Mohammed Abdi

To the women and men who showed us the way!
To all the rebels, who fight for democracy and emancipation!
To the women and men who perished for our freedom!

To Chakir, August 2006,
In recognition of the warmth of your welcome in Morocco,
which allowed us to finish this work.

To those who are close to my heart and who share in my struggle.

Fadela's Origins

I was born in Clermont-Ferrand. I am Auvergnate. My parents are Algerian immigrants with residence permits, but I'm French.

My father came to France in 1955 for economic reasons. The poverty in his village in Kabylia was extreme, and he had trouble finding "regular" work. Exploited by the colonists, he decided to leave. When he got to France in 1955, he went to Clermont-Ferrand, where a family member was already living, an uncle who has since passed away. My father moved to Clermont-Ferrand alone. Unlike most people living in Clermont at the time, he didn't go to work at Michelin. Instead he went straight into construction work. You might say that he contributed to the creation of Clermont: the streets, the new buildings and factories under construction.

My father is a construction worker who never learned to read or write. He has admitted to us that when he first came to France, he was paid fifty cents an hour. As kids, we would laugh when he told us that. We couldn't believe it.

At first he slept at the worksites because there was no housing set aside for immigrants like him. Unlike my brothers and sisters, I have always been able to get him to talk. My father is a very reserved person, someone who doesn't talk much. So to get him to talk, you have to be patient, really patient. When you finally get him to open up, he expresses things that are painful, but he always does it in such a calm, serene way. He talks about coming to France under difficult conditions, for economic reasons. Deep down, he already knew that he didn't want his children living in conditions of almost total poverty.

He comes from a village called Ait Youssef in the mountains of Kabylia, where there is absolutely nothing—no school, nothing. He lost his father when he was very young, and for a long time after that he was a shepherd. Unlike my mother, who learned French thanks to a Jewish family who took a liking to her, my father never went to school. He had never held a pen in his life. Later, we made him pick up a pen so that he could learn to write his signature. He learned to sign his name, but that's all.

My father possesses the kind of intelligence that is common among people who don't read or write. Maybe by instinct or for survival, they develop a very practical type of intelligence. I've noticed this in working as an activist alongside immigrants who haven't had the opportunity to go to school: when they look at papers and bills, they pick out colors and acronyms. They manage to pay the bills and pass out letters among the family when they're the ones who pick up the mail. In immigrant families there are generally lots of children, and despite everything, a father who neither reads nor writes can distribute the mail without making mistakes.

My father arrived in France in 1955. He slept on cement sacks, taking three or four of them without the boss knowing. It was hard for him to ask; he didn't speak French very well. Even today he still speaks broken French. So he slept on cement sacks when he arrived, though later he got up the courage to tell the overseer of his construction site, at that time a Portuguese guy, that he had nowhere to live. The overseer went to see the boss, and the boss gave him this little storage room, the place where they hung their coveralls during the day. At first he slept in there, just like many immigrants who came from North Africa.

Then, eventually, he found a place to live. He moved in with a French woman and lived with her. He doesn't talk about this time very much. The only way I know about it is through my mother. My father wouldn't have told me because that kind of thing just isn't talked about in my family; everyone is very modest. It didn't work out with the French woman, and he went back to Algeria in 1960 and married my mother, who was then fifteen years old.

My parents are twenty-two years apart in age. It was a marriage negotiated by the families, which was a common practice at the time. My mother was a young girl who had lost her mother very early on, at the age of four. Her aunt raised her because her father had left Algeria to move to France. My grandfather lived in France for a long time. He made a new life there and has since died. My mother stayed by herself with her aunt in Algeria and was raised with her cousins.

My grandfather, who made a very poor living in France, didn't send any money back to his family in Algeria. They began to say that he had abandoned them, because life was really hard in Algeria for a poor family—extremely poor—living not very far from Algiers. Those were rough times; it was the period of colonization. We're talking about people who were living under the Indigenous Code, true indigenous people, not like those pretenders who call themselves that today.[1] They were the true indigenous people of the Republic, and that meant they had no rights, absolutely none. They worked, and they were dependent on the colonists, the bosses who had moved over there and who hired them on a day-to-day basis, without giving them a work contract or even a pay stub.

At one point, we tried to reconstruct my father's work history in Algeria, for his retirement. He started working when he was eleven years old, and he didn't arrive in France until he was thirty-eight, but everything he had done before coming to France had disappeared. He doesn't have a single document from Algeria to prove that he had worked since he was a child, absolutely nothing. The colonial archives show no trace of his work life; they didn't even record his date of birth. My father told me that at the time, there were no labor contracts or pay stubs. You were paid under the table. It was that way for years.

At the age of fourteen or fifteen, my mother had financial worries. My father, who is one of her cousins, a member of the extended family—in fact, they were born with the same last name—was in Algeria at the time. To help pull her out of poverty, he asked to marry her. They were married in their hometown, and then he brought her to France right away, the very next night.

My brothers and sisters and I, we were all born in France. My father has known my mother since she was a baby. My grandfather is my father's first cousin. He's barely older than my father, five or six years at the most. They're from the same generation. My father saw my mother grow up. Every year when he came down to Algeria [from Kabylia], he saw her. She was a sweet little thing, as they say. I would guess that he married her out of a sense of obligation, but that's just my impression; they aren't the ones who told me that. He married her out of a sense of obligation because she had been abandoned, and so that she wouldn't wind up on the streets in some sort of terrible situation.

It was an arranged marriage. I think the love came later. Today they're inseparable. They've had eleven children together; one of them died in my

1. The Indigenous Code [*Code d'indigénat*] was established by the French in 1881. It established a separate judicial code for Berbers and Arabs in Algeria, effectively creating a two-tiered society of citizens and "subjects." Indigenous Jews in Algeria were granted full French nationality by the Crémieux decree of October 24, 1870, and were citizens until the revocation of that decree during the Vichy regime. An 1889 law made French citizenship automatic (unless it was specifically rejected) for all children born in Algeria of non-French European immigrants. —Trans.

mother's womb, and two others have died since. Because of all the hardships they've experienced and the ten living children they've had, my parents are really close.

For example, when my mother's not around, my father doesn't talk. You can really tell that he needs her there. Even though they bicker constantly, they're inseparable. My mother does exactly the same thing when my father isn't there. Every time they get mad at each other, she says to him, over and over, "Old fart! You're just an old fart!" But they always make up in the end. And for his part, during arguments he always says, "If you keep that up, I'll go looking for someone else in Algeria. I'll replace you!" A banal phrase, followed by silence. My father would say it just to tease, but the threat was hardly veiled. My mother, like all women, learned how to live with this sword of Damocles hanging over her head.

When I was small, this shocked me, and I was afraid that my father would leave. Now, little by little, the love between them has grown, and all the blows that we have survived have have completely brought them together. They have managed to get through everything: prison, death, everything. That has really united them.

I think that, as is true of many couples who have come from abroad, the experience of living in France, of suffering rejection, exclusion, and racism, has truly helped them find the strength to resist. The very fact of having succeeded in building a family in France, of having raised children in an atmosphere of extreme exclusion, of having lost all their rights, has given them courage and dignity.

My parents were placed in shantytowns when they first arrived as a couple, because someone had suggested that they live there. After that, they were shuffled around, geographically stigmatized, because everyone knew that only Arabs lived in this or that camp or shantytown. Finally they moved into a housing project in the Herbet neighborhood in Clermont-Ferrand. At the time, it was supposed to be temporary housing.

Back then, there were no working-class people in that neighborhood, no native-born French who were living the same hard life that we were, although today there are. Back then, the neighborhood wasn't mixed. When I was born, 99 percent of the people in the neighborhood were of Algerian origin or from the northern Maghreb. Essentially, then, I grew up in an Arab, Algerian village. At most, there were two or three French families who lived in the neighborhood. They were old, very poor retirees, who were as destitute as we were, but for the most part it was Arabs, Algerians.

Later the sociological composition of those neighborhoods evolved and included low-income French families. Starting in the seventies, as poverty began to touch everybody and unemployment hit both whites and Arabs, the social fabric unraveled even more.

When my family arrived, things were really wretched. As a family, we had been shamed and humiliated; we lived in complete fear of the authorities. My parents, like the majority of immigrants of their generation, have always feared cops, authorities, uniforms. When I joined the fight against racism and antisemitism, my parents were terrified that the cops would descend on the house to take me to the police station. That's why when there were police raids in the neighborhood, my mother would shout: "Quick, quick, the paddy wagon [*panier à salade*] is here!" What a funny expression! Except that we knew very well what it meant, in terms of suffering for the family, when the police came to arrest someone. This fear of everything that authority represented encouraged my parents to "hug the walls."[2] My father, like many others, participated in the war during the German occupation; however, the years these men spent in the army did nothing for them and did not give them the feeling of being integrated into the French nation.

At the time, Algeria was divided into three French departments. When my family arrived in France, they were treated like dogs, not on the same footing as other French citizens, white citizens, for example. Later they went to war for Algerian independence. They made a choice that I respect and admire. It was important to fight for a people's right to self-determination. Often, in evoking this dark time in our history, my parents' generation, sparing in their use of words, make it clear that they needed to tighten their belts to help win independence. Bearing the hope of an entire people, the struggle for Algerian independence was also waged by the women and men of France, some known, some anonymous, men and women whose courage in the service of this noble cause contributed to its victory. This is the France that I try to represent in the battles we fight today, and I hope always to live up to this ideal of justice and equality.

This is why I remain scrupulous about the perception that people have vis-à-vis the Algerian war. We need to be careful today not to confuse what we experience in the housing projects with the true Indigenous Code to which people were subject and under which they lived. The co-optation of a history, or its interpretation, is a suspect business. It can be made to serve ideologies of exclusion and seems to me quite dangerous; I cannot accept this. No one has the right to co-opt the history of our parents and distort it to serve political interests. I think that's despicable. My father was humili-

2. The expression here is *raser les murs*. Literally meaning "to shave the walls," it indicates an attempt to remain unnoticed or practically invisible. This strategy for getting by renders immigrants even more marginalized. —Trans.

ated, and when I speak of my father, through him I am also thinking of the Algerian people. Everyone lived under a terrible system that deprived them of their rights, with the exception of the Algerian bourgeoisie, who, thanks to certain privileges, lived somewhat better; they had access to education, for example, with which they could arm themselves intellectually to organize for independence for all the others (peasants, shepherds, workers, the illiterate); it was very difficult.

What they lived through over there, they lived through again here in France, even after the war of independence. They endured the same humiliation. When we were born, we children, our parents instilled in us the desire to return to our homeland, and since they viewed themselves as having immigrated only for economic reasons, the assumption was that we would not settle permanently in France.

I grew up with this idea in my head, this famous "myth of the return." My father absolutely wanted to go back to live in Algeria, the land of our ancestors. This wasn't anything shocking: I understood it, and my mother understood it, too, although she was more aware of the difficulties it would involve. We could see that it would be somewhat complicated, but then this myth, this dream, was shattered when we realized that we couldn't move back and live over there. We didn't speak Arabic, and furthermore we were Kabyle in origin, which made everything that much more difficult.

We nonetheless remained strongly attached to our homeland, to our history. So why did they teach us at school that the Gauls were our ancestors? We weren't idiots after all!

The twists and turns of history, whose puppets we are, often aren't recorded and taught as they should be. Each to his own task, and I'm of the opinion that it's the historians' job to shed light on historical facts, and not the job of politicians to spout their "historical truths." Seeing my own life framed by the destiny of humanity, it matters to me that the memories of each group become my memories, too. So it is with the memories of the Shoah, of the African genocides, of countries in the East and elsewhere, and so it is with a people's struggle for self-determination. We must all contribute to the construction of the collective memory for which "never again" has meaning and reality.

Beyond the creation of an immigration museum, it's important to teach and transmit the history of immigration in our country. The part that foreigners have played in the construction of our country, in its economic and cultural development, has to be recognized if we are going to change the often negative attitudes that some people have toward foreigners. People don't emigrate for pleasure, but most often out of necessity. This kind of rupture demands a strong personality to withstand the unknown and hold up beneath one's share of suffering.

This is why so many of my generation admire our fathers tremendously; unlike the third generation, we have enormous respect for our parents. First, because we lived through their suffering with them, but also because we imagine what they lived through before we were born, and we recognize the mistakes we made. To be sure, there was racism; but we know full well that for many of us who didn't succeed for *x* or *y* reason, we have to bear part of the responsibility. Our situation was difficult, perhaps even more difficult than it is today, but racism doesn't excuse everything. That is why I loathe the discourse of victimization disguised as generosity. In reality, this discourse doesn't urge those who suffer racism to live together with others; rather, little by little, it pushes them to the side to live in submission and abandonment.

The suffering endured by our parents when they emigrated—leaving their country, leaving their families, coming here to an unknown land—the sum of this suffering remains a forgotten part of our history that hasn't been recognized either in France or in our homeland. And we've been at a loss as to what to do with this suffering; we haven't lived up to our parents' hopes. And they never reproach us for it, which is even more terrible.

Many children in my generation failed in school, or they didn't do well. Even those who studied, who fought for it and struggled like crazy, and even succeeded in getting a diploma, they haven't been recognized or accepted or integrated just because they are Arabs. Back then, to be Arab meant to be excluded. It still does, but less than before because now there's a middle class that has emerged from immigration.

At the time, it was very difficult to find a real job, and we didn't know how to make the most of the suffering of our parents by pursuing advanced studies and succeeding no matter what the cost. Our generation was brought up to succeed, regardless of the price that had to be paid, and even if the problems we encountered and the context of the times made it particularly difficult. We have to remember the seventies and eighties, which were terrible decades economically and for the way they used Maghrebi immigration. My father and many others like him strangely thought that because we went to school—the school of Jules Ferry, the school of the Republic—we would become full citizens and upwardly mobile. For them, the idea was to make enormous sacrifices so that their children wouldn't have to belong to their same social class or be at their same level, and above all wouldn't experience the same suffering and humiliation, stripped of their human dignity. They fought hard, getting up at five in the morning, returning home at eleven o'clock at night.

My mother never worked; my father wouldn't allow it. He was very severe, very strict in his upbringing. He was clearly living with the legacy of a patriarchal society. Women, in his opinion, were meant to raise the children; men's duty was to see to the family's needs. The man must fulfill his responsibilities, no matter the cost. This extremely traditional division of labor seems to him to this day the only valid one. But only for his wife, not for his children. He accepts that society has evolved. But with respect to his wife, no, he'll never admit it; he'd never agree to my mother working, for example. Even though he recognizes that raising children is a full-time job, he was nonetheless astonished that my mother was entitled to paid retirement. When we submitted her file, he kept saying, "It's not true, they aren't going to give her retirement!" I said to him, "She raised children, and since she raised French children, she certainly does have a right to retirement." He couldn't understand it. "I worked like crazy my whole life and I'm entitled to nothing at all, so why does she have the right to retirement?"

I pointed out, "You could at least say: fortunately she'll get retirement, because she raised your children and she worked her whole life, too!" But, in fact, I understood that what offended him in the case of my mother's retirement payments was that she would have resources of her own at her disposal. She would have a little financial independence after the age of sixty. This was unbearable for a man who had been raised in a patriarchal (indeed, even tribal) society.

My mother arrived in France in 1960, after she married my father. She had her first child in 1961. My parents told me nothing about their marriage. There's no photo, no trace of the wedding; it's as if it has been erased from time. My mother, who clearly had no idea what awaited her, told me one time that on the day of the ceremony, she found herself in a room with the whole family. They told her she was to be married. For her, it was a simple thing, obvious, and above all the only means of moving forward in life. They didn't have any money; they belonged to a poor family, indeed very poor. Furthermore, it was 1960, before the independence of Algeria, and the context was confusing and difficult. My father never told me about his marriage, though I certainly asked several times, but my attempts were in vain. Finally I succeeded in learning that before my mother, he had married two other women. He spoke of them sometimes and explained, without apparent guilt, the reasons why he had repudiated them: it was their fault, period. This was normal in a patriarchal society, an extremely severe society, extremely masculine, where women were practically nonexistent. By contrast, he still refuses to talk about his marriage with my mother.

My mother was young, so he had a great deal of authority over her. When I was younger—she had me when she was nineteen; I was the fourth child in the family—I recall her playing with us, like she did when she was a child. We threw a ball against the wall, up to three, four balls; we juggled. I remember my mother running and having fun; when we jumped rope, she jumped into the circle, even when she was pregnant. I have many images from my childhood in which I see my mother young and pregnant. I always envision her pregnant, because every year she gave birth.

In my family, the last children are one and two years apart, and there I take it that Simone Veil, a great woman for whom I have enormous respect, had been heard, and that above all my mother had secretly disobeyed, certainly with the aid of our social worker at the time.[3] Because my mother didn't go out. Like all the Arab women, she stayed at home, she didn't budge. When my father said "Stay put," she stayed put, because otherwise there was a chance she'd be smacked.

There was a kind of respect instituted, but by terror and fear. It is really disappointing that these archaic practices still exist in some families. In certain neighborhoods today, the same attitude can be seen among the young men, but it's a thousand times worse because they don't have the excuse of having been conditioned by a patriarchal society. They've grown up here, in a "free and equal" society, and that makes all the difference.

Our mothers, as a result, didn't go out. They stayed at home; they had coffee with each other and told their little stories. My memories of my mother are of her playing, being pregnant, being home. And I see my father, with a gap of twenty-two years, who seemed so much older than she was, so much more aged. My brothers and sisters and I were all truly afraid of my father; he inspired immense fear in us. He almost never spoke, but when he did, you'd better run. He spoke only to reprimand us, because we'd done something stupid, because my mother had told him that ten kids are hard to manage. But now she always says that she'd rather watch ten kids of our generation than one of today's kids.

My mother thinks that young people today are savages, that they've become terrible and insufferable. As for us, she tells us that when we were little, we weren't naughty, we were well-behaved and obedient. Though I must say we had a very strict upbringing. For example, my sisters and I didn't start leaving the house alone until we were twenty-five years old. I really mean

3. Simone Veil was the minister of health from 1974 to 1979. She is best known for her fight to make contraceptives more widely available and to legalize abortion. —Trans.

alone, because at twenty-one, our father still went with us everywhere, even to buy pants or clothes.

It was only later that we began to go out. I had begun my rebellion before then: I skipped school, missing class, on the sly, just to have a little space to breathe, and above all because I didn't accept this sort of supervision. We were watched all the time by my older brother, who was extremely severe, especially with me, because I had a big mouth and was a real rebel.

Boys and girls were brought up differently: the boys had more freedom, more choice, although my father was still strict with them. They had a curfew they had to respect, but they could come home from school later than the girls. The girls had to come home immediately; they weren't allowed any space: when they left school, they had to go directly home. When the boys got out of school, they could have fun outside in the housing project before they had to come back home. They had places where they could have a good time and amuse themselves; we had less.

When my father was absent, my mother gave us permission to go out. We would play with the boys in the neighborhood. Together we played cops and robbers, cowboys and Indians. Space in the housing project was still mixed. We grew up together, we fought, but only over trifles, the troubles of kids, and we were all mixed in together. Some of the boys who saw that we were playing with other boys were jealous, and they intervened. But they were never allowed to hit a girl directly; they would see us and say, "Just wait until I tell your brother!"

The brother played an important role. Today I think a lot of these older brothers in Maghrebi families have snapped. The pressure put on them when they were still kids themselves was really too much, especially because the rest of society didn't operate by patriarchal laws. They would have had an easier time playing by everyone else's rules.

We breathed the air of French society even if we were closed in, in every sense of the term. Being born in the sixties, and growing up during the seventies and eighties, during the boom years, even if it never crossed our own thresholds, the general climate was permeated with it. Outside, I saw women working, I noticed that the elementary school was directed by a woman, I saw that women occupied roles in society and in public life. I was dazzled by the new trend that gave women the chance to work for a living, indeed even to excel in certain domains formerly reserved only for men.

My older brother, for example, had a really strict upbringing, but at the same time, what our parents asked of him was extremely difficult because they didn't give him the keys he needed to understand. He was asked to play the role of a cop in relation to his sisters even though he could see that in society at large, women had the right to go out, the opportunity to do things. He had to find a middle ground. Now, how can we ask a boy of ten, eleven, or even fifteen or sixteen to play this role and take on this responsibility? It is really complicated. My father wanted him to be in the Algerian army, so he left to join the army. It was very hard for him. Just as my father lived through hard times when he immigrated and lost his old identity, my brother lived through hard times in Algeria, where he was treated as a dirty Frenchman. He no longer knew where he was or who he was. He crossed a line when he came back; he did something really stupid, and he was tried and sent to prison for a long time.

I think that for the second generation of immigrants, conditions were really difficult: they had boundless admiration for their parents, and at the same time they could see that their parents were obliged to hug the walls and lower their heads before an authority who instilled fear in them. Then we turn up, suddenly we're there; we go to public schools, and we're taught liberty, fraternity, equality, even though our social situation is terrible.

We understood that we didn't enjoy full rights, that all of that wasn't true, it was a lie: rights had to be wrested away, they weren't given. We quickly became aware of the need to fight to create our own space, taking account not only of the values of the society in which we lived but also of the values of the families to which we belonged. The two had to be continuously juggled.

Many in that generation said they felt like they had a foot in two worlds. During their adolescent years, a number of them had terrible identity crises, which had lasting effects for some of them, leading for many, notably girls, to catastrophic ruptures with their families. The boys also paid a high price. How many of them became drug addicts, died from an overdose, or went to prison? Because they lacked a space, a place where they belonged, a fixed point of reference, their identities exploded. Neither one nor the other, they didn't know who they were or where they came from. And in order to go forward, you have to know who you are and where you're going.

For example, the lack of guidance with respect to the public realm—the lack of social mobility, at any rate, for many—gave rise to a generation that was wounded and hurt. The solution for many of us was to become political activists. Others fell into delinquency; still others took refuge in their studies and fought hard, and for some of them it worked out, while for others it didn't. But in the eighties, many of us were engaged in the fight against racism and for equality, which gave rise to the March of the Beurs. There was a whole generation, the children of immigrant parents, who became involved, not with mainstream politics at first, but with the activist struggle for republican values. For us, this marked the beginning of our desire for resistance and recognition.

This struggle, the fight for these values, had also gone on inside me since my childhood. My father's upbringing, the example of my mother, public schooling, all these helped to forge my identity. I feel like sort of a patchwork; I am still and always will be under construction. I am still not finished; I am still absorbing influences today; I am always in process. And the foundations of the person I am and aspire to be were laid in the way my parents brought me up and the values they transmitted to me. If today I defend freedom, equality, and respect for human beings regardless of their origin, that is simply because in my upbringing and education, from my earliest childhood, I was taught the importance of this principle.

When we were small, my father categorically refused to allow swear words or insults between us brothers and sisters; it was forbidden in our house. If we insulted one another or grew angry with each other when my father was at work, my mother would report it to him in the evening—she felt obliged to. Our father would call us together in the kitchen or the living room. It was very solemn. He made it official, set the scene, took us through a whole ceremony, as if he were putting us through a ritual that was going to help us remember this moment so that no child would forget it. He would stand in the living room waiting for us; he would place us together face to face, the two protagonists, and ask us why we had quarreled. Each gave his or her version, and then he made us apologize to each other, kiss, and ask for the other's pardon. He would lecture us, explaining that life was difficult, that he hadn't had the chance to have a father, or to be raised in a "normal" family with a papa, mama, brothers, and sisters, and that he had had to go to work very young. For him, brothers and sisters, family, were like the fingers of a hand, together able to stand up to violence, to all the problems from outside—he would say this in Kabyle. He explained: "You, the brothers and sisters, and the family must be like the five fingers of the hand; you must be inseparable. Each of you lives his or her own life, but you confront problems together, and when one of you falls, everyone has to help and support that one."

My brothers and sisters and I were raised this way. No doubt this is why, even today, we're extremely attached to one another and support each other. When one of my brothers or sisters is with me and has a problem, we immediately start to look for a solution. Even today, we remain very close. Of course, everyone has their own character; some of my siblings are more sensitive than others, but truly, we really support each other. So when something bad happens to one of us, everyone runs, everyone is concerned, and my mother acts like an Italian mother, possessive and often intrusive. You only have to see how she behaves when one of us falls. She only has us; she's given everything to her children, sacrificed everything for us, like many Arab mothers. As soon as one of us is sick, as soon as one of us is far away—and we almost all have cell phones—I don't know how she manages it, it's totally irrational, but as soon as one of us isn't well, she feels it. She calls and says, "I know it, so you don't have to lie to me," and you feel obliged to tell her the truth, to tell her that indeed you are sick, and she responds, "I know, I saw it." It's impossible to lie to her, even at a distance; it's incredible, and she rushes over to take care of us.

Public school made me who I am. Besides the upbringing given to me by my parents, I was strongly influenced by this notorious civics teacher, whom I initially detested. He was very strict, with his gray apron and unpleasant expression. He was like a cartoon character. He came dressed like a teacher from the Third Republic, and he entered the classroom carrying a switch, which he set on his desk just to draw attention to the punishment, although the threat was stronger than the actual execution. He was very tough: when he gave his lecture, you'd better listen, and participate, all the way to the end. If he ever pointed his finger at a student, asking him to come to the blackboard, that student had better answer. The Republic, the history of the Republic, the foundations of the Republic, the values of the Republic, he crammed them into us through our noses, mouths, and ears. I hated that teacher. I know he's dead now, but I honor his memory because he's the one who made me love the Republic and its values; he's the one who taught me to love democracy.

When you're a kid, you don't feel like democracy has that much to do with you. It was only later that I understood the importance of democracy, that is, that every person, regardless of his or her sex, lives in a democratic society thanks to, by, and through the possibility of self-expression via the vote. At that point you understand what freedom is, and you see, or become aware, that it isn't a luxury, that it should be natural but it isn't. You understand why you have to fight against any form of oppression that might arise, both where you are, in the country where you live, and also throughout the world, in terms of solidarity.

There is no fight more important than the battle for human rights: that someone can choose to say no or has the right to do so without being subject to pressure or suffering oppression. Here in France, people don't always take this into account, because we are a fairly affluent population, and a bit capricious; but that civics teacher taught me these lessons for life. Now I know that it was he who helped me become who I am, in spite of myself. In my mind, I know that he is at the core of my fight against injustice, that he prepared the ground for the fight I lead today. His lessons often come back to me in memory; I always go back to what he said. I think about him when I'm in the middle of things; even when I made my Tour de France I had flashes, images of him saying to me: "Fadela! We all have to be there to defend the Republic and its values!"[4] When we engaged in debates in the evenings on the tour, and were faced with hundreds of people, I spoke and saw his image. It's incredible how the word "Republic" works like a flashback, leading me back to the situations I lived through as a child.

When I was little, the school I went to wasn't mixed, although it later became so. At the beginning, the boys were on one side, the girls on the other. Several years later, I was part of the generation in which boys and girls were beginning to be mixed together in school. I began in a preschool and elementary school that weren't mixed; then the elementary school became mixed, and we girls were put together with the boys. For us, though, it didn't change much.

Our school wasn't just a dumping ground, as is the case with some housing projects today; it was still really a sanctuary. School takes on a crucial importance in my eyes. We knew that it was through school that we could pull ourselves up; we were keenly aware of it, especially since every day our parents repeated to us: "Pay attention, you have to work at school, you have to stand up straight, you have to eat right."

I have to give my mother credit. She got up at four thirty in the morning to light the fire that my father had already laid. He then left for work at five o'clock. We didn't have heat at home; we used coal. She would take care of my father, making his coffee, preparing his breakfast and a lunch to take with him. Once she had finished with him, she would wake up all the children, then wash them without a shower or heat.

We were a clan of ten children in a tiny apartment, three rooms above, two below. The four daughters in the family slept head to foot in the same room. This afforded us some good laughs, and a few general brawls, too, but the lack of privacy left us with good memories in spite of everything. This might seem strange since we were so poor; I can only appreciate it now, when I see the difference from life today. I realize that our parents really played the role of parents; that is to say, they protected us from the awareness that we were poor and that we couldn't have everything we should have. My mother played an extraordinary role; like a lot of mothers, she was one of those women who

4. The reference here is to the March of Women against the Ghetto and for Equality, which Amara organized in February 2003. The march mimicked the famous Tour de France in moving to a housing project in a different city each day, covering most of France's major cities in just over three weeks' time. —Trans.

sacrifice themselves. She always found a way for us to eat correctly, even if I can remember sometimes not having had my fill. But our parents managed so that we didn't realize that life was hard, or have a sense of life's difficulties.

When I look back, and I often talk about those times with my brothers and sisters, we just see a big, warm sun when we return to childhood in our memories. We see kids with patent leather shoes, little dresses, ribbons in their hair. My mother was crazy about that stuff; she treated us like dolls, and I, for one, hated it. It was a headache every time she did my hair, and besides, I always had problems with my hair. My mother was really strict about cleanliness, and that annoyed us, too. In the morning she got up and washed all ten children, which wasn't easy, since someone had always wet the bed and it was cold; the conditions were difficult—it was a shantytown, after all. This was before the renovation and the famous bathtub that made the task easier for us. And my mother, an extraordinary woman, she always managed to have everything impeccable; she did everything, washed everything, by hand. I remember her washing the linens outside; there was no washing machine. It was crazy: she washed the diapers by hand. I recall when my other brothers and sisters were born, there were no disposable diapers; only my last brother, Malik, had disposable diapers, because he was born in 1973.

Before his birth, I remember mountains of cotton diapers inside the house. And in winter my mother hung up the diapers inside to dry. I remember my mother being hardworking, industrious, a real stickler for hygiene. For example, I was a rambunctious child, a bit of a nuisance; I played a lot of boys' games, I was always running around in the yard. Where I lived, in the Herbet neighborhood, there were large fields where nothing had been built yet; we played cowboys and Indians there. When I came home, I was always filthy; at school, I seemed to always have a head full of lice. I was the one in the family who got lice and passed them on to everyone else. My father didn't like women with short hair, that just wasn't done, so my mother could never cut my hair. There was always hell to pay with the lice comb.

My mother was deathly afraid that someone would say she was incapable of raising her children. I remember the day of the nurse's visit at school, my mother was afraid the nurse would write down some criticism in her notebook, it didn't matter what it might be. She couldn't bear it; her children had to be irreproachable, healthy, clean. She was uncompromising about hygiene, almost obsessive; even now when she comes to my apartment, she does a round of inspection, criticizes, and makes comments. And me, I say: "Listen, Mama, I try to do what I can, I don't have the time." For her, this is just an excuse.

Any time she stays with a member of the family, she goes around and inspects. Of course, she won't say that it's not very clean, but I know it, I'm used to it, I know how she operates. If it isn't really clean, she'll get up at five in the morning and clean the whole house. There's no use telling her to stop or to take it easy, or promising that you'll clean it more the way she likes; she won't relax. So, fine, I admit that my place is a bit messy. I have books scattered everywhere.

When we were small, she would get up before us, she would take us to school. We would form a chain holding her hand, four or five behind her, and she would keep an eye on us, a little like a camp counselor. As there were about fifty wives in the housing project, they were almost all heading to the same school, and they would talk among themselves, each of them pulling along a chain of kids by the hand. We were lined up from biggest to smallest, or sometimes the reverse; we changed it around to break the monotony a little. At a certain point, my eldest brother got fed up with being made a fool of, as he put it. So he left for school along with the other boys from the housing project.

My mother took us to school in the morning and came back to fetch us at midday, because we didn't eat in the cafeteria; it would have cost too much money. Then she would take us back again at the beginning of the afternoon, before coming to get us again at the end of school, around four thirty. When we had a little more money, from a government family allowance, she was able to pay for school lunches. She wanted this since on the one hand she was snowed under with work (notably with washing the sheets we kids had peed on all night long), and on the other hand she knew that it was beneficial for us to eat in the cafeteria, since it meant that we could avoid the round trip at midday, and we could eat a well-balanced meal. She always managed to buy the first fruit of the season when it came in, even if we didn't have a whole lot of it. She would put money aside; she wouldn't hear any argument about it. Her children had to taste the first cherries, the first peaches, the first apples. It was always like that. For example, yogurt was a luxury for us at the time, and she took money, in secret, from my father's pocket to buy it for her children. She did the same with candy. She would buy things only for her children; I never saw her buy anything at all for herself, not a dress, not jewelry. We were the ones who bought things for her later, once we had begun to work.

My mother was born outside Algiers. She was abandoned by her father, she had lost her mother, so she was raised by her aunt, which was difficult even though she adored her aunt. Her uncle and aunt brought her up the hard way. She was lucky to have as neighbors a Jewish family who became fond of her. She still talks about them today; she would love to find them again, but she doesn't know how to go about it. This Jewish family wanted to adopt her. They called her Fifi; my mother's name is Zouina. When she was a girl, she often went to this family's home to visit; she would eat there, often staying until late in the evening, and then they would bring her back home. The mother of this family wanted to send my mother to school. But it wasn't possible to do it because my mother had to stay home and take care of her half-brothers and sisters. She regrets it, and still talks about it from time to time. "It's too bad; I should have been adopted by this family. In fact, I would have liked for them to adopt me, because then I would have gone to school, I would have become a doctor." And I would say: "If you had done that, you wouldn't have had us!" We would joke about it, but I could see that she still found it hard to swallow; it was like an open wound that was still painful. Even in her little bit of free time, I would see her sigh when we sat next to her reading books. How many times did she tell us how lucky we were to know how to read and write, if only so that we could escape by reading? To say nothing of escaping the shame that comes from having to ask someone for help when you have to fill out administrative forms. We were too little to understand. It's terrible to live with illiteracy, and in spite of everything, even today we have people who cannot read or are practically illiterate. What a mess in a modern society!

This Jewish family made a profound impression on my mother. It is impossible to talk to my mother about antisemitism; she doesn't know what it is, she doesn't understand. Yet there are stock expressions, in our everyday language, that demean Jews. It's so common that hardly anyone pays attention to it, even though it's an antisemitic expression. When I explain the scope and the seriousness of these stock phrases, I'm often told, "It's nothing, it's just an expression." That may be, but surely we are also faced here with a banalization of antisemitism.

When my parents watch a film on the Shoah, they get upset. My mother goes through four boxes of Kleenex; she can't bear it, can't accept it. When she speaks of the Vichy period, she insults the French, calls them collaborators. She often tells me that antisemitism hasn't weakened in France, that this mentality hasn't gone away, that there are still traces of it, and with its own words and vocabulary, it remains hidden but powerful and terrible. I agree with her; I know she's right. If we had eradicated antisemitism during the last war, no one would even speak of it today. But it has made a strong comeback in certain neighborhoods, where the young people, especially children of immigrants, take everything out on the Jews. The Fofana affair, among others, is unfortunately a good example of this.[5] My mother can't

5. This refers to the 2006 kidnapping, torture, and murder of a twenty-one-year-old Jewish man, Ilan Halimi. Youssouf Fofana, the alleged leader of the plot, admitted that Halimi was targeted solely because of his race. Fofana was sentenced to life in prison, the most severe sentence permitted by French law. —Trans.

understand it, since for her we are all in the same mess, the same world, and it's in all of our interests to extend a hand and fight for equality and justice so that no other children are humiliated. And she knows what she's talking about; she has experienced racism, she knows what it is to be humiliated, scorned because you've been categorized, and stigmatized just because of your foreign origin.

Though when you see my mother, with her white skin and blue eyes, it's difficult to tell she's a foreigner until she begins to speak. She still has a strong accent, even though she speaks fluently, whereas my father still speaks broken French today.

During my childhood and adolescence, I often listened to my mother and her friends from the housing project who came to our house. I learned an enormous amount from those women as they spoke of the problems they had encountered in their lives. I'd buzz around them, asking to stay; I drank in everything they said, these women, these mothers, trying to understand why the boys were so protected and the girls so disciplined and constrained.

I became conscious of my condition as a woman very early, around the age of eleven, if not before. Why so young? Because at eleven years old I went from primary school to junior high, and it was like a slap in the face. I became conscious of being a girl. Of course, I already knew that I was a girl, and that I was different from boys. It didn't bother me because it was the norm, the rule that was applied identically to every family in the neighborhood. All of a sudden I woke up. I had crossed a threshold when I got to junior high. I met other girls besides those in my neighborhood. They told me about parties. I had no idea about parties. They explained that they celebrated their birthdays, that they threw parties at home, that they could go to sleepovers, all things that weren't allowed for us. Even within our own neighborhood, it was unthinkable to sleep over at a neighbor's house.

I was already beginning to make comparisons between how boys and girls lived within my own family, but also more generally between how all the boys and girls lived in my neighborhood. I could tell there was a difference; I saw very clearly that there was something strange. It was even more striking in my own family, because my father was considered the hardest man in the neighborhood. He was very strict with his children, and particularly with his daughters, extraordinarily demanding. If we ever slipped up, and for him no matter what girls did they were slipping up, things would get tense very quickly. For example, if I was even fifteen minutes late, he would immediately get angry at my mother, just like all the other men in the neighborhood. It was always the mother's fault: she was too lax, she didn't punish enough, she didn't watch her children closely enough . . .

It was my older brother's job to watch over us. At first it was voluntary, and he gave in to whatever my father wanted. He thought it was fun to wield this authority that gave him status in the family. I would have huge fights with him, and he would often slap me. We had a difficult and turbulent relationship, especially when I was an adolescent. But later he made some mistakes. He was arrested, tried, and sent to prison. Prison helped raise his consciousness. Throughout this whole family drama, I was really hard on him. Despite everything, though, I didn't abandon him. He's my brother; we have the same blood. I had no pity for him, and at the same time I took advantage of the fact that he was locked up so that we could meet every fifteen days. I wanted to settle the score that I had not been able to settle before when I was too young and he would always pull away from me. Those meetings, spread out over several years, really helped to bring us together. Most of all, they helped me understand why a boy would suddenly turn into an oppressor at the request of his family, in the name of honor. This code of honor does not visibly apply to boys, no matter what mistakes they make; it is applied exclusively to women. My other brothers did not feel this pressure; it was reserved for the oldest brother. It's strange how this concept of the "big brother" has come back full force in the past few years thanks to policies intended to instill social peace in at-risk neighborhoods. By this means, a patriarchal system has been reintroduced that has become the norm, much to the detriment of girls.

Faced with this terrible situation, I shouldered the responsibility of my family, torn apart by suffering. I replaced my oldest brother. I changed my status. I took charge of the whole process. Basically, I tried to handle all of the family's problems. Since then, my father says that I am not one man but ten men. Coming from him, that is a huge compliment. In Kabylia, when a man touches his moustache and pulls on it, making a face as if he were going to pluck it all out, that actually means that dishonor will come to the person he is talking to. When he spoke about me when I was an adolescent, he would often reach up and pull on his moustache as if to say, "Fadela, dishonor is going to come to the family through her."

Today he doesn't want me to be criticized, and he tells anybody who will listen that "Fadela, she is ten men." He knows the price that must be paid for freedom. He doesn't say it, but I've heard from my mother that he worries about me. The fight against obscurantism has plunged so many families in Algeria into mourning that everyone today is conscious of the value of freedom. My father's words, which come from the heart, are extremely important to me. It shows how proud he is of me despite his fear. My father speaks only in metaphors. He doesn't speak normally; he comes from an oral culture, like all Berbers. He often expresses what he thinks by quoting the great poets, such as Si Mohand ou-M'hand, and by commenting on common proverbs that he uses to explain situations. But when he repeats to me, admiringly, that I am worth ten men, I slip in a few words just to tease him: "You could say ten women!" For him that doesn't mean anything; women are always beneath men. I have tried and tried to explain this to him, but every time he retorts: "Yeah, yeah! I get it, but you are worth ten men." In his head that is his point of reference; he is still marked by, steeped in, conditioned by patriarchal society. He does not understand. It has not hit him yet. He also does not grasp why I strive to understand: "You and your politics, always trying to understand everything," and I say to him: "No, Papa, you have to think of men and women as equals."

When I was little, I used to ask him questions in broken Kabyle: "Are men and women equal?" He would respond: "Of course, but women in the home and men outside." If a man doesn't live up to his responsibility as a father by providing for his family, then he is not a man. If a woman doesn't take on the responsibility of raising the children correctly, if she does not play the "role" that the man as the father of the family has ascribed to her, then she is not a woman. It has been hard to sort through these ancestral notions.

When it comes to his children, it's another thing entirely. When people talk about us, his girls, and about me in particular, he says: "Let today's youth do as they please. They go to school. They work." But his wife is his possession. You can't go there; it is not up for discussion. He gets angry very quickly. He is extremely jealous of her. It's a different situation when it involves his wife. He knows that women's rights exist, but not for his wife. He is the one who decides there. It's incredible the number of men I have met, from different social and geographical backgrounds, who acknowledge what they put their companions through, but who pay this reality little more than lip service. (And by the way, I am not singling out young men from tough neighborhoods, I'm talking about men in general.) I'm taking it upon myself to say it, even though the truth is sometimes difficult to hear.

The collective unconscious contains a lot of stereotypes. For example, many people think that women in Muslim or Arab societies play no role or only a submissive role. In reality, when someone begins to study how the family unit functions, taking the time to understand its mechanisms, it becomes clear that the pillar of the home is the wife, the mother; she holds everything together. Everything depends on her abilities, her intelligence, the extraordinary survival instinct she has developed because she has been considered a minor since the dawn of time. And when I see Arab or Muslim mothers act and react, I admire them, notably for their ability to make their husbands or the men they live with believe that they [the men] direct the family, when really the men direct nothing at all. I've often seen and heard women say, especially when they came over for tea or coffee, "I was able to do this because I said that." I had the impression that it was a game of chess and that they were masters of the art of manipulation. They play the game strategically to get one thing or another. They advance, they retreat, they seem to be on the other side, but what's important to them is whatever is real, the objective, the result. And they often get exactly what they set out for. It's a veritable feminine counterculture with its own rules and customs. These women don't hesitate to pass along information or the best way of doing something. There is real solidarity among them. From the outside, at first glance, it might seem that this is a patriarchal, tribal way of doing things, where women are ceaselessly humiliated and disgraced, their rights ignored. We have to let go of our Western prejudices to see that this view may be slightly wrong. Things are not so cut-and-dried, even if they aren't formalized. You can see that in the way Kabyle society functions, particularly among Berbers, where the woman's role remains very important.

Nonetheless, it's unfortunately true that women have been deprived of their rights. On the question of the veil, for example, people often say that Kabyle women do not wear the veil, but they are the ones who work in the fields while the men chat in the village square. They are happy because they are outside, but they are exhausted!

One of the essential political struggles, for me, is to achieve recognition of a mother's place and role in society. Progress requires that mothers benefit from a formal status. They must be officially recognized—*all* mothers, including those not of North African origin. Values and traditions are transmitted through the mother, and in certain immigrant families she is also, unfortunately, the means for the transmission of oppression in the form of archaic traditions that are coming back full force today. Using the tools of emancipation, we must enable mothers to attain a position of dignity, but they must also be afforded the power to change things and to modify the cultural norms that were transmitted to them through their own upbringing.

Is it possible in the housing projects today for a mother to tell her daughter not to wear the veil even if her husband demands the opposite? Yes, but either she will say it off the record or, if she really loves her daughter, she will say it openly. And to defend her no matter what the cost, she will do whatever it takes to make her position known in order to fight the battle. At the same time she knows that, unfortunately, her fight can go no further than the marriage contract. In the marriage contract, girls have the status of minors, even if they are asked ahead of time. For example, if we're talking about a girl who gets married according to Muslim tradition, contrary to what is often described, the imam is obligated to ask the woman, to seek her consent. He must be attentive and verify that she is not being pressured before the marriage, not by her father, her brother, or any other male member of her family. The imam can and should ask questions. Seeking consent is important for the future husband, too, because there are arranged marriages for men as well. Only after that consent is obtained can the religious marriage ceremony, which is called the *fâtiha*, go forward in front of witnesses and the family. A man does not immediately represent the woman who is getting married. She must say yes, and then the imam can address the male family member who represents the young bride.

In the housing projects it still works like this today, even though there were relatively few religious marriages in my generation. Religious marriages have come back full force over the past few years. In my day there were many more civil marriages; today no civil marriages take place without the religious marriage happening first. Before it was merely ceremonial, because the few religious marriages that occurred took place in the prayer room or in the mosque. Actually, this was called an "engagement ceremony," even though it was a religious marriage. The woman stayed in her house with her family. The men, who prayed and went through the religious marriage ceremony, were elsewhere in the prayer room.

Increasingly today, religious marriage has become something highly official that takes place in front of the community. In my day, only a few families did it. Later, many families wanted to "go back and make things right," thinking that it was not enough to have a civil marriage, that a religious marriage was also necessary. So in the housing projects, there was an increase in the number of ceremonies that took place seven or ten years after the civil marriage. If you are married religiously, it's clear, all is well. Today the pressure on families is getting stronger and stronger. In the housing projects, as soon as people find out that you're not married religiously, they come straight to you, saying that it's not a real marriage. In their words, you are "living in sin." Practically everyone in the neighborhood then singles you out; everyone points a finger at someone who is not married religiously. In certain neighborhoods, it's the same thing for girls who don't wear the veil. They are pointed at; they are pressured, insulted, harassed. And it has just as much to do with their peers as with religious or institutional networks. It is often peers, neighbors, friends, but it's also the organizations with an archaic, *intégriste* Muslim bias that have established themselves in the housing projects.[6] We used to call it

6. See fn. 13 in part I on *intégrisme* in the "Special Assembly of Women of the *Quartiers*." —Trans.

"basement Islam" [*l'Islam de cave*] because they worked in darkness in order to keep people in the dark.

This movement began in the mid- to late eighties, but the real tipping point was in the nineties. When they began, they found an inroad through language, in extremely insidious discourses and sermons that became more and more radical on the subject of women and girls. By "they," I mean imams, but self-proclaimed imams; nobody else recognized them as such. Many of them had come to France illegally, some from Belgium, Pakistan, the Middle East, etcetera. Many were funded by Islamist organizations, such as the International Islamic League. Others came from Algeria or Morocco, as distinct from those who are commissioned and officially sanctioned by the governments of those countries. These imams spread their message everywhere, including our housing projects. Their way of thinking, transmitted to the young boys who attended the sermons, most certainly had an unconscious effect on the boys' behavior toward girls. Everything started in those housing project basements, little by little.

Yet parents' attitudes at that time had evolved tremendously on the question of girls. In those days, it was expected that girls would go to school, and they were allowed to go out from time to time in the evening, even if they had to be supervised and accompanied by their brothers. A girl could choose her clothing and wear makeup, and it was becoming increasingly possible for her to choose her husband. This explains the higher number of mixed marriages back then. When I talk about mixed marriages, I am not talking about young women like me, the child of immigrants, marrying a guy from the home country. No, these were girls or boys of foreign origin who would marry French whites. Today mixed marriages are forbidden. This is a big and worrisome step backward, because at the same time arranged marriages are on the increase, notably marriages within a single community: among the Senegalese and people from parts of sub-Saharan Africa, among Algerians, Moroccans, Tunisians. It is even becoming complicated among people of Maghrebi origin for Moroccans to marry Algerians, for example. Today we are living in a veritable state of regression.

When the *intégristes*, these self-proclaimed imams, started preaching in the basements, you could see the boys in at-risk neighborhoods, especially those who felt distressed or confused, change their behavior. Most of them ended up turning away from it pretty quickly—*intégriste* practice is extremely rigorous, and they didn't stick with it—but others continued to be pious, and I respect that choice.

What has fundamentally changed today among the new *intégristes* is their intellectual capability and their determination: it's no longer the young people who are disenfranchised, failing school, or searching for an identity who join, but young people with five years of higher education and the capacity to think systematically. Some of them study medicine, engineering, or computer science, and yet they hold to an inflammatory Islamist discourse. It's a dangerous situation. We have gone from one problem, which I would call sociological—and which was linked to economic difficulties and problematic behavior—to a political problem. This is one reason, among others, why my thinking evolved on the question of girls wearing the veil. In 1989, I supported it so that girls would be allowed to stay in school. Republican schools transmit the tools for emancipation and cultivate true citizens, capable of being free and forming their own opinions. I made a mistake. At the time I minimized the impact of religious obscurantists. Their power to strike is real, and it's linked to their ability to organize. In certain neighborhoods it's hard to get away from them, especially when you are a woman. There was such pressure that it became difficult for the school to take care of the problem by itself. Thus we went from two to several hundred girls wearing the veil. We were no longer dealing with girls looking for an identity, or simply going through an adolescent stage, but we were dealing very plainly with a part of our youth living under the pressure of a discourse that instrumentalizes religion. This discourse is propagated by associations, magazines, and Internet sites.

We have said it over and over again: the absence of a strong political response to the problems in disadvantaged neighborhoods has made conditions ripe for the emergence of an increasingly fascist discourse. On one side is the extreme right, and on the other its corollary, Islamism: allies, in practice, though not intentionally, in favor of political agendas in which the status of women is almost exactly the same.[7] From hard-won emancipation, we are sliding toward total regression. The veil has become the symbol of a political vision that brings with it gender inequality and separation of the sexes in public spaces. The pressure exerted on girls who refused to wear this symbol of oppression was unbearable. Many of them ended up giving in because they could not find sufficient support. They ended up orphans of the feminist movement. This is why, during the course of the republican Tour de France organized by the Ni Putes Ni Soumises movement, I realized that we must put a stop to this disastrous progression.

My first thought was that we should come together around the value of *laïcité*, as the founding value of a vision of society in which we all share a

7. Amara is making a distinction between Islam, the religion, and Islamism, which denotes when the religion is instrumentalized for political ends, be they those of the far right National Front Party or those of fundamentalist or *intégriste* forms of Islam. —Trans.

common space while individually respecting the different groups to which we belong, whether these be social or religious groups or simply groups linked to sexual orientation. To encourage popular support for French republican values, Ni Putes Ni Soumises proposed to the Stasi Commission that we should organize debates throughout 2004, all over France, to include all the pertinent social and political figures in the country. The grand finale would be a huge popular festival celebrating the hundredth anniversary of the law of 1905.[8] It turned out not to be so simple. *Intégristes* from all sides howled, and their representatives demanded that we rethink the whole concept, adapting the idea of *laïcité* to take into account new sectors of the population and their beliefs. Even worse, some who consider themselves part of the fight for progress supported this move in the name of "the right to choose." What "right to choose" are we talking about here? Where is the right to choose when the conditions aren't there to allow one to choose peacefully, free from outside influences? Above all, can we speak of the right to choose given all the forms that we know pressure can take and when we know that certain people won't hesitate to use this pressure to gain ground, expecting to win the battle against democracy? Have these progressives become deaf and blind to all these signs that point to the worst should we fail to act?

In reality, on top of everything else, the evolution or rise of *intégriste* discourse has accelerated the deterioration of conditions for women in the *quartiers*. We find ourselves in a situation where the most threatened, the most oppressed, populations are girls—and also homosexuals, because there is extreme homophobia in these neighborhoods. We know it today, even if it's difficult to talk about it publicly. With Ni Putes Ni Soumises, we have managed to break the silence about girls, and also the few boys, who have suffered violence. But with few exceptions, we still have very little testimony from the young homosexual men who have been subjected to punitive attacks and barbaric rapes. Being recognized and designated as a homosexual makes life unbearable for certain young people in the housing projects. They haven't been given concrete help because homosexuality is still really difficult to talk about openly. Even more than with the girls, it's difficult for these boys to open up about the suffering they endure.

We often end up with the same kinds of struggles. There is a frontier that, though virtual, nonetheless exists and encircles the ghettos, turning them into pockets of neglect to which people are relegated. On the outside, beyond that frontier, we have to fight for the emancipation of individuals, for their rights, using organizations that are effective at the grassroots level and a

8. Instituting the separation of church and state. (Author's Note)

civil society that remains ever alert and ready to struggle against all forms of exclusion. The attempt to extract these rights, to win the rights guaranteed by the constitution, nonetheless conflicts with the reality of the current situation, because the legal mechanisms in place stop at this imaginary frontier. In these little circumscribed pockets, girls do not have rights, and neither do homosexuals.

There is an entire cross-section of our population that is completely forgotten. So we must get back to basics. This is why, for example, on the question of feminism and parity, which is one of the only demands made by feminists in the past few years, I used this phrase which certain colleagues took the wrong way: "Parity, for me, is like going to a sale at Hermès." The girls in the ghetto and the women in rough neighborhoods were fighting to survive, and those from the outside were talking to them about parity. We can agree on the principle of parity, but where I live, in my dilapidated neighborhood, it goes right past me; it's just a concept. For the moment, I'm just not there. I still have to say: "Attention, everyone, I want to dress however I want. I want to live however I want. I want to have the right to control my own body." This is why our movement fights first and foremost against the regression of girls' status and women's conditions. In the future I might say, "Let's go ahead with parity!" But I'm not there now; I'm nowhere close. Some feminists did not take this well, but not all; the majority supported us right away. They understood that feminists had failed in trying to shrug off the social question, as well as in not managing to pass on everything that the feminist movement had accomplished.

I think that Ni Putes Ni Soumises today permits us to clear some feminists of any suspicion of guilt, especially those who have been strong supporters and have really helped us. We have learned a lot from them. We have fed off their experiences; we consider ourselves a bit like the heirs to their feminist and antiracist legacy. And yet, at the same time, we see the relationship as a sort of apprenticeship, because with a few exceptions, many of their gains were not concretely passed on. Our movement wanted to be the bridge that allows these two worlds [feminism and the ghetto] to come together, to mix, to share each other's struggles. We transmit the values that disadvantaged girls need in order to really participate in feminist struggles, including the fight for parity.

In many at-risk neighborhoods, young boys and girls have interiorized all the tools of oppression. The discourse of victimization has become dominant. It must be dismantled, but it is not easy to initiate grassroots action. Despite everything, however, more and more girls and boys from these neighborhoods are rising up and declaring themselves "Ni Putes Ni Soumises." Three years later, we are beginning to see increased awareness. People are beginning to speak out more freely; perspectives are changing. There is a new dynamic. We are turning things around: the majority, previously held hostage by a visible and active minority, has begun to mobilize, and we are beginning to see visible changes that inspire hope for the future. A changed power relationship is developing step by step. It's complicated, though, very difficult and extremely fragile . . .

Mohammed's Origins

I was born in East Morocco, in Oudja, a city on the border with Algeria. My village was called Naïma and had the notable feature of being built around a train station from the colonial period. The train passed through once a day; if you missed it, you had to hitchhike to get to Oudja.

In my mind's eye, I can still see the women who waited for the train, silent, unassuming women covered completely by their haiks.[1] They hid their faces each time a man passed, as if they were apologizing for existing.

I was born into a polygamous family and spent my childhood in a large house built around a courtyard. I lived with my father's wives and my brothers' wives, under the authority of my father, a property owner who was well respected in the region. My father's family fought over political power and territory with another large family in the area.

I was the child of my father's last wife. Until his dying breath, my father kept his first wife, my adoptive mother. She was the one who protected me from my father's frequent fits of rage. He always kept three or four of his wives next to him. My father repudiated my mother when I was still very young. It wasn't customary at the time, but according to the law, custody of a child remained automatically with the father.

So I grew up separated from my mother, living with my father's wives, truly in an emotional no-man's-land. The children of the first wife were given much more consideration than I was; everyone looked on me as a forgotten child. I had no news at all of my mother during my whole childhood. My

1. A haik is a large piece of silk, wool, or cotton cloth worn as an outer garment in Morocco. —Trans.

father raised me with his other children, in a sort of community where I had to make my own way to survive. There was plenty of everything in the house, and often an abundance. However, the principle of equality didn't exist, and I was excluded from the favors bestowed by this wealth. In that house, a kind of injustice prevailed in which people received consideration in this order: my half-brothers, then my half-sisters, then finally the others. "The others" meaning the employees of the house, the cousins, the rest of the family, not to mention the tribe, and then me. Excluded despite the wealth, marked by the memories of my childhood, I was haunted, deep down in my heart, by a sense of the injustice of what I had lived through since I was small. This was how my revolt was born. In this large house where many women lived, the organizing principle was above all masculine. I lived this way until I was seventeen years old.

I don't remember having big dreams as a child. Existing, for me, was a misfortune. I was one child too many; no one paid me any attention. There was more affection on my stepmother's part than on my own father's. I never thought, during my childhood or adolescence, that one day I would be lucky enough to go to France to study. During my whole adolescence, I lived my everyday life without a horizon. I didn't understand why I was in the world; I just was, that was it. I didn't have a room of my own, and I felt excluded. Can a person ever recover from exclusion? It's based on insurmountable things. With poverty, you can overcome it, but exclusion is a sort of wound buried deep inside oneself.

Then, with my diploma, I began to realize that I wasn't all that bad in school. I didn't have to be first in the class; no one asked that of me. I often did poorly on my homework on purpose. My professors knew it; I was their favorite. It was as if they understood that I was required to fail.

In adolescence, my father, who had family in Oujda, sent me to live with one of my half-brothers to pursue my studies. Little by little I forged my own freedom, notably thanks to the theater course at my high school. And my Arabic professor, a known activist, invited me to meetings of the young socialists. At the time I had no political convictions, and I felt very isolated. We would meet after school, in semi-secrecy. It was there that I learned the essential facts of the history of Morocco. Our lengthy discussions allowed me to understand what I resented, the injustices I observed in Naïma, and to put words to what had disturbed me: patriarchy, exploitation, submission, inequality, injustice . . . I was not the son of a poor man, but I felt excluded. As I learned the names for things, they began to be clarified.

But our approach to the struggle wasn't unanimously shared. In fact, another organization, Chebiba el Islamiya, "the young Islamists," was extremely active. Confrontations were common, and the violence intensified when one of the socialist leaders, Omar Ben Jelloun, was assassinated by an Islamist activist in Casablanca in 1975.[2] This episode was decisive in forging my convictions and my commitment to freedom and democracy.

After I got my baccalaureate, my French professor, Madame Carpentier, recommended that I go to France. I felt like I was on probation; I had no dreams. I arrived in Paris alone, without any money, in 1981. It was a Saturday evening. I flew into Orly and was really surprised by all the shops inside the airport. I got a taxi and told the driver to take me to the city center. He responded: "Which city center?" I admitted to him that I was lost. He explained what I could do and offered to drop me off at the university residence halls for international students. On the grounds of the residence halls, I encountered an Iraqi who led me to the house for Morocco. They took me in, and I was quickly able to establish connections with other students. They were my tribe, my network, like a new family for me.

But in order to get to Clermont-Ferrand, where I would be enrolled in the university's Department of Economics, I had to leave Paris. I left on a Corail train, changing at Saint-Germain-des-Fossés, with just a two-minute stop. Everything seemed strange, the gray weather, the stations without anyone on the platforms, the absence of light, of movement; I felt like a stranger, alone in the world.

Then I arrived at Building B of the Étienne-Dolet university residence halls in Clermont-Ferrand. The smoky, activist ambience of the dorms impressed me immediately. From then on, everything was amazing. It was a paradise, a rebirth for me. I saw neither racism nor discrimination. In the main hall, there were pamphlets calling for strikes and for changing the world order. Those texts attempting to save the world filled me with joy. It meant that there were people who wanted to stand up for the fate of the weakest. Every evening, people gathered in the name of different causes; it was a veritable marketplace of ideas and struggles. There was a meeting for every cause.

I realized that I had left a world where everything went unsaid, where political expression was illegal, and I had discovered a place of *mixité* in which energies were liberated. I was a student, a member of UNEF.[3] I had always been interested in meeting people who were different from me. I was impressed by the determination and activism of some of the young people,

2. Omar Ben Jelloun was stabbed to death by Abdallah Muttii, a cobbler on his estate who was an activist with Chebiba el Islamiya. (Author's Note)

3. UNEF is the Union nationale des étudiants de France. It is the primary union in France that protects the rights of students. —Trans.

especially the women. I fell in love with a girl who was strikingly intelligent and was taking the prep class to apply to France's most elite universities. I was ready to do anything to impress her. She shared with me her passion for reading. I began devouring books, just to be able to talk with her, to be at her level. This was a turning point for me and gave me a center of gravity. Dazzled by this love, I wanted all the women in the world to be just as freely intelligent; that's how I became a feminist.

I was equally amazed by the bouillon cube and the cafeteria flan that I devoured.

I had a scholarship, but in order to live, I also worked at a crêperie four nights a week. I was the first Arab to work at this crêperie, and the boss was so fond of me that she invited me to spend Christmas with her family. For the first Christmas, my boss set a grand table. That really struck me, all this formality—since childhood, I had always eaten in a rush, surrounded by noise. It was the first time anyone had offered me foie gras; I had never eaten it, I thought that it was paté!

Everyone else working at the crêperie was homosexual, those who worked in the kitchen as well as those who worked in the dining room. It bothered me. This was the first time I realized that I had prejudiced attitudes. Later, when I read Marguerite Yourcenar, I understood that your true homeland is that place where you see yourself clearly for the first time.

Clermont-Ferrand quickly became my adoptive city. I came to know every detail of the city, the center as well as the outskirts. I was surprised to find in those outskirts the same thing that had appalled me in Morocco: the injustice and exclusion that some people suffered. The old foreign workers housed by unscrupulous slumlords; the interminable lines in front of the Immigration Administration [*commissariat*] to get the famous residence permit [*carte de séjour*].

The March for Equality in 1983 and the creation of SOS Racisme were what revealed, for me, the general disquiet that extended well beyond the neighborhoods of Clermont-Ferrand. It was my first political engagement, and I was still quite young. I met Harlem Désir and Julien Dray.[4]

4. Harlem Désir was the first president of SOS Racisme and remained at its head from 1984 until 1992. He is a longtime member of the Socialist Party in France and is currently a member of the European Parliament. Julien Dray was another of the founders of SOS Racisme and subsequently made a career in politics as a member of the Socialist Party. He was elected to the lower house of the French Parliament in 1988 and has remained in office since. He is currently under investigation on charges of embezzlement related to withdrawals of funds from SOS Racisme and the Independent and Democratic Federation of High School Students (a group he also helped to found). —Trans.

The image I had of a beautiful France where no one had to struggle to survive began to crumble. So I took part in this movement for equality and emancipation. I met Fadela Amara at the offices of Asti (the Association for Solidarity with Immigrant Workers). Her devotion and her boundless determination impressed me. This girl, whose parents were from the Maghreb like me, who had lived in a shantytown on the outskirts of Clermont-Ferrand, racked by racism and machismo, who had experienced exclusion, this girl didn't see herself as a victim or feel humiliated. She simply wanted to change things. This attitude of hers has always impressed me.

I began to take more and more of an interest in her struggles. But when Fadela put out the call for Ni Putes Ni Soumises in 2003, I hesitated to follow her. I thought she was wrong and that the social question was more important than the question of women's status. I was a prisoner, trapped in a discourse of political correctness. I quickly came to understand that the dominant political discourse didn't account for what was happening: the violence in the *quartiers*, the increase in veiling for women. But still, I was shocked by the name "Ni Putes Ni Soumises." Fadela held out, and she was right: it was necessary to strike hard. I became totally committed to struggling alongside her, and Sohane's death definitively confirmed my decision to fight against this surge in sexist attitudes, which found its justification in an Islamist discourse resting on an ideology of victimization.

I know that Fadela's the real thing. She has been forged by hardship; she has put her life on the line; and her start in the movement was very difficult. She was quickly and violently attacked, but she didn't crack in front of people, she never caved in. Some people took her for the Madonna of the *banlieues*; others found her unsettling and irritating. We are at a point in our movement where we have to find the frontier and hold to it. Our fight concerns what is to come, the future, living together, removing the stigma from the *banlieues*.

The movement has been in existence for three years now, and we are everywhere: in America, in Quebec, in the Near East, in the Maghreb, and of course in Europe. Everywhere, Fadela is received like a dignitary; she had the distinction of being awarded a doctorate *honoris causa* from the Free University of Brussels in 2005, and in July she will receive the same distinction from the Manchester Metropolitan University. Fadela invited Malika Oufkir to accompany her to the ceremony, along with some girls and boys from the projects outside Paris. Fadela, who has always regretted not having had the time to pursue her studies, wearing her cap and gown there on campus, cried with joy because she had been awarded the title of doctor. Her life has changed a lot; she wanted to be a star, but she thought she would never make it.

Fadela loves her country; there is something irrational in her connection to France. She thinks that she can pardon it for anything; she is French from head to toe; sometimes she's even a little too patriotic, a bit of a flag-waver. After a time, I came to understand her attachment to her country. In her mind, she has constructed a France as beautiful as a dream for all humanity. Even if she feels racism and exclusion in her flesh, her profound love for France stops her from making a negative judgment. When Fadela says "my country, my republic," it isn't rhetoric. It is love anchored in the most profound part of her being. She is one of the women and men who have made me love France.

Immigration

Fadela

In France it unfortunately seems to have become the case that if you have nothing to say or propose to the French people, you talk about immigration. And every time, it's an effort to set things right again.

At the moment, I'm working with women whose lives have been complicated by their illegal status. Some of them are married to legal residents of France. Some are married to legal residents and also have a child born in France. Over the years, many of these women have tried to sort out their situations. They go to the prefecture and end up being shipped off to the Immigration Administration to be deported.[1] That's how it goes. Some of these women were able to contact us with the help of someone close to them, or in some cases it was a local association that brought their case to our attention. It's a little bit difficult to know the extent of the harm caused by such situations, even in my own city of Clermont-Ferrand.

With the help of the lawyers who assist us, I am trying in my own small way to work directly with the minister of the interior on those cases that appear particularly serious from an administrative perspective, but even more so from a humanitarian one. Some of the women involved have a child born in France who is still very young. If they leave, life will become difficult because the child will be left with the father. I think it's important to organize

1. There are one hundred *préfectures* in France, one for each of France's regional departments. The *préfecture* is the administrative office in charge of identity cards, driver's licenses, vehicle registrations, passports, and residence and work permits. The prefect is the chief administrator of a French *département*. Among other duties, the prefect acts as the chief of police for all local police departments in his or her administrative territory. —Trans.

things in such a way that these women are able to stay in France with their children and get a residence permit, which will bring them peace of mind. It's a legitimate request, and I don't think this form of legalization goes against public opinion. I certainly hope that no one throws "public opinion" in my face, because a common retort from the ministries is that "public opinion isn't there yet." The idea is to reduce the red tape for cases involving the wife of a legal resident, because these are women who could, in any case, gain legal status on the condition that they return to their country of origin and then come back to France a year or two later within the framework of immigration laws designed to allow family reunification—although this status, too, is harder and harder to get.

It seems to me that a fundamental individual liberty is being tampered with here, namely, the right to live together as a family. The political situation of these so-called foreigners seems to me paradoxical: suppose, for example, that tomorrow someone just like me, the child of immigrants, decided for completely personal reasons to vacation in her parents' country of origin, and suppose she fell in love—one never knows where or when the heart will impose itself. Given the new laws, it would be extremely difficult for this woman to bring her spouse back.[2] This touches on a very important freedom. We no longer have the right to choose whom we will marry. If he or she lives in France, that's fine, but if it's someone living elsewhere, we're told that with this very rigid law we do not have the right to choose. This is terrible. I don't like this trend.

There is a question that worries me and that I regularly ask myself: What would the left do if it were in power today? After all, the left was in power, and what did it do to improve the lives of these same people? Not much. Faced with the current attitude of resignation and confusion, when many would have us believe that there is no real difference between the left and the right, I remain firmly convinced that for the sake of political debate and democracy, the division between the two sides is vital, even if I think that neither has a monopoly on good sense.

2. France passed a new immigration law on July 25, 2006, which took effect in 2007. It aims to encourage highly skilled immigration while placing new restrictions on the immigration of low-skilled or unskilled immigrants and on immigration for the purpose of family reunification. The law also further limits access to residence permits and citizenship. At the time the measure was passed, about 65 percent of immigrants to France came into the country under the mantle of family reunification. According to Nicolas Sarkozy, then minister of the interior and the architect of the 2006 law, France made a mistake in 1974 when it shifted from worker-based immigration policies to family-based policies. The new law was designed to help return the country to a worker-based policy. —Trans.

I expect French values to be otherwise and understand them otherwise. For me, France is the incarnation of a country of immigration [*terre d'accueil*]. I'm not a fan of overly utopian discourse, and I know that France has to manage its migratory fluxes. But I think it is possible to legalize the status of those without papers [*sans-papiers*] who have been in France for a long time and whose children are in school here. I am fighting against the current course taken with respect to young high school and middle school students who have no papers.

The Education Without Borders Network (Réseau éducation sans frontières), a support organization, was created through sponsorships. I understand that the government finally gave in and agreed to legalize some of these young children who were enrolled in French schools, thereby, in a ricochet effect, agreeing to legalize the status of their parents as well.[3] But what will happen to all those who were not born in France, who arrived here too late according to the ministerial circular, or who don't meet the requirements even though they've received almost all their schooling here? They won't have a place to live anywhere . . . In their case, we've largely made a mockery of the principle of equality. And to be deported, what a terrible beginning in life!

I think that France, our country, is capable of legalizing the *sans-papiers* who have been here for a long time, who have built a family here, who have social links with their surroundings, and French friends. I encourage this legalization. Spain was able to do this with between 700,000 and 800,000 foreigners without papers.[4] I think the 150,000 in France can be absorbed. Many of them work under the table and are exploited. I think their situation can be legalized without it being fatal for the economy, because they are already in the system, although in a way that harms them. They are exploited, notably in construction jobs, restaurant work, and also in agricultural industries that employ migrant workers. Their employers must be forced to declare them.

3. In 2006 there were an estimated 200,000 to 400,000 illegal immigrants in France. The government set a target number of 25,000 deportations for the year, but met with severe criticism in late spring over several highly publicized cases in which families with school-age children who had been in the country for many years were deported. Public protests spurred the minister of the interior to grant a temporary amnesty to families with children in the public school system. Families with such children were then eligible to apply for legal residency, although only some 6,000 adult slots were made available. —Trans.

4. Spain, with a population of roughly 40 million (compared to France's 61 million), awarded legal status and residency papers to 1 million illegal immigrants between 2000 and 2004. It legalized another 570,000 immigrants in the first half of 2005. Gregory Viscusi, "Deporting Children from France May Cost Sarkozy Votes (Update 2)," August 8, 2006, http://www.bloomberg.com/apps/news?pid=newsarchive&sid=az5iuEPqsIoo&refer=home (accessed August 24, 2009). —Trans.

In order to fix this problem that is poisoning political life, we should legalize, with certain conditions, all those who have created a family [in France]. Then we should develop immigration policies, which should be designed for and with Europe. We should seek a coordination of laws that allow for generosity. Even if some say that there are things that will not work, we are in a position of strength and we should be generous. The idea would be to develop a generous approach, so as to welcome individuals who bring their strength and intelligence to our country to develop our economy, and at the same time we should develop policies of cooperation with the countries of emigration. This logic of reciprocal relations, of constructive cooperation, of simultaneous economic development in two countries based on principles of equality and in a relationship of equality—where one country doesn't think of itself as superior to the other, where one doesn't think for the other—all this will permit a new politics of development. In this way, people will develop a taste for and a desire to stay in their country of origin. If things are going well at home, they will not come here except as tourists, and we will be happy to welcome them as visitors to France!

I am skeptical about controlled immigration. Since this would mean, in the first place, choosing a certain type of immigrant to the detriment of others. De facto, it would be as if there were a vast market of immigrants where each country could do its shopping. Once a selection is made, a country closes its doors. But you can put up all the walls in the world, and it still won't affect people's determination to flee misery and poverty. If I were living in a poor country, in which my family and I were dying of hunger, I would do everything to save the lives of my loved ones and others I knew. Thus it strikes me as useless to establish hard and fast policies that restrict people's ability to obtain a residence permit. We should take the global nature of immigration into account, with all that it represents. Let me stress this point: people do not immigrate for pleasure. The vast majority of people who immigrate leave home because they have no other hope of finding a way out, economically or politically. Some flee corrupt regimes in which poverty is endemic. Women are on the front lines. Today, more than 50 percent of migrants are women. This feminization of migratory fluctuation is a new and growing phenomenon.

The idea would be to develop a more intelligent management of migratory fluxes, taking into consideration immigration in its new and global dimension. In effect, immigration doesn't only concern rich countries. Developing countries are equally concerned. They are faced with migratory fluxes that are increasingly significant. Today, besides its 26 million native residents, the Ivory Coast counts more than 6 million foreigners, thus more than 26 percent of its total population. In the Gulf countries, immigrants make up a third of the population. This phenomenon also exists in countries such as Algeria, Morocco, and certain Asian countries. In the years to come, a number of other countries will face these issues as well. Hence the necessity of rethinking the question in a more global context that eventually integrates the question of codevelopment.

Unfortunately, persistent prejudices stop us from incorporating these new facts and keep us from having a complete and coherent view. In France, people think that immigration is the source of all our problems: crime, unemployment, etcetera.

I am not a scientific researcher, but from where I stand, the high rate of unemployment in at-risk neighborhoods doesn't seem to be directly linked to immigration, and still less to clandestine or illegal immigration. In my humble opinion, it is the prejudices, discriminations, and self-censorship by certain directors of human resources when it comes to hiring youth from the housing projects that seem to account for the elevated unemployment rate. In the High Commission Fighting Discrimination and Promoting Equality (Haute autorité de lutte contre les discriminations et pour la promotion de l'égalité), of which I am a member, it is noticeable among the numerous appeals.[5]

We must completely dissociate the issues of unemployment and immigration. Immigrants have jobs just like everyone else, and that's a good thing, at least for those who have residence permits. Some who work in construction, seasonal work, or restaurant services have jobs but no legal papers. Should we then punish those who work without papers? Wouldn't it be better to legally and financially punish the owner who employs them knowing that it's against the law? There's a problem: certainly, those who come into the country illegally have no right to work, but at the same time, do they really have the possibility right now of legalizing their situation? Obviously not.

The illegal immigrant is never alone. He has a wife and children. Attacking such a worker also means attacking his family. The family link and the choice to live as a family are elements that have to be taken into account. The French feeling of solidarity with school-age children who have no papers shows their attachment to this right.

The right to live as a family, to bring one's family to one's principal place of residence, is of utmost importance. Workable and relevant programs would enable everything to be ready when an immigrant arrives, including programs

5. The HALDE is France's independent administrative authority charged with combating discrimination. It has powers of investigation and recommendation, but no direct judicial authority. —Trans.

aimed at literacy and learning the language of the host country, with specific courses on the history and values of the country. In exchange, the immigrant needs to engage with and respect the rules and laws of the welcoming country. The right to housing remains an additional basic element of the process of integration. This is why I have always fought against approaches to housing that, in order to keep certain sectors of the population out of the center of the city, build apartments there with just two or three rooms. People pretend that anyone can live in these apartments, but in reality people know that most immigrant families are large, and this is a way to clear them out of city centers. It's a means of selecting the people who will live in the city center. So on top of the economic question—and rental prices are frightening—people find a way to exclusively build housing that will accommodate only three or four persons. This is what we'd call a discriminatory policy.

With respect to the fight against unemployment, the biggest shock for me has been hearing about and seeing the figures for executive packages. I think that people who take on large responsibilities should be paid in a manner commensurate with those responsibilities, especially if they're in charge of the economy or the politics of the country and in order to avoid corruption; after all, if someone has important responsibilities, it's important that his or her salary reflect this. But I find it indecent that the heads of large companies, in addition to their enormous salaries—consider that in my whole life I may never see even a third of what they earn in a month—receive severance pay when they leave. On one side, there is this system of golden parachutes; on the other, there is a witch hunt for so-called "false RMIstes."[6] And yet we well know that these people live in situations of real financial insecurity. Perhaps there are some frauds, but we shouldn't generalize on the basis of the two or three who have defrauded the system. We chase after those who have an RMI worth three or four hundred Euro—one wonders how they can even live on that today—while no one seems shocked to hear about these other transactions, in which the amount of money, millions of Euro, is so astronomical I don't even dare speak of it. I don't see laws being put in place or politicians standing up to say that it will be necessary to curb this system of injustice, even though it is extraordinary and enormous. I think there's a profound injustice here and that the money in question could do

6. "RMI" stands for *Revenu minimum d'insertion*. It is a special government unemployment benefit available to those who are at least twenty-five years old or have children and who are not currently students or in a job training program (among other qualifying restrictions). An RMIste is someone who collects unemployment benefits under this plan. —Trans.

more good if it were invested in a business where it could be used to hire more people and fight unemployment.

I feel that the immigrant, with his residence permit, is not viewed as a citizen like the rest. The residence permit, this awful piece of paper, allows him to remain in the country. He is recognized, he can present his card when the police demand it. He can live quietly and doesn't have to slink along on the margins of society, but he is marginalized all the same as long as racism and discrimination exist. Not all French people are racists. And yet the mounting populism throughout Europe gives rise to fear. In my eyes, the 21st of April, with Le Pen in the second round of elections, wasn't an accident but rather a profound sign that something worrisome is happening in our country.[7] We need to pay careful attention to it. I'm always afraid of the rumblings of fascism, the sound of boots on the march that you hear in the distance every time there's an economic downturn. We find ourselves in such a situation today, with depressing, defeatist, anxiety-inducing talk fueling people's fears. I feel that politicians respond negatively to the subjectivity of our fellow citizens. There is incessant talk about crime, and it gets associated automatically, as if by chance, with the word "immigrant." Together, these two themes are like a bomb waiting to explode.

I believe that manipulating the debate—notably during presidential elections—by choosing these two themes is a lie, a true hypocrisy on the part of our men and women in politics. Of course crime and insecurity are to be feared; that is a reality. But the greater fear for people is unemployment. Regardless of which social class you belong to, when you have a child—boy or girl—you worry that he or she won't be able to find work, even after completing a long course of studies. For fathers and mothers, this is the greatest source of worry.

For some years now, violence has been on the rise in the housing projects, and with it a feeling of insecurity. I believe that the people in the projects

7. The first round of France's 2002 presidential election took place on April 21. Polls had predicted that the top two finishers would be Jacques Chirac (running for the right-wing party, the Rassemblement pour la République, which later became the Union pour un mouvement populaire, or UMP) and Lionel Jospin (then prime minister and a member of the Socialist Party). Instead, Jean-Marie Le Pen of the National Front edged out Jospin and made it to the second round of elections. Le Pen's campaign focused on crime and insecurity, as did Chirac's, but under the inflammatory rhetoric of "French First." Le Pen said that his first priority would be to protect poor white families threatened by North African immigrants in housing developments outside France's major cities. Le Pen was overwhelmingly defeated in the second round of voting on May 5. —Trans.

have the right, like everyone else, to security. They have the right to live in peace and to go about their business without fear or threats. The principal problem surely remains the fight against unemployment and financial instability. That constitutes the greatest fear of the French today, and I believe that our politicians offer few solutions. They prefer to avoid the real issue and feed people's fears, taking the risk that the noise of boots on the march will increase, rather than trying to bring all the actors together at the same table to find solutions.

We need to reflect on what happened in 2002 and neither forget it nor treat it as an accident of history. I believe that during presidential elections, the immigrant is invoked to manipulate public opinion. The immigrant with a residence permit certainly has legitimacy, but when we are in a difficult period, there is a tendency to demonize and stigmatize a certain sector of the population: we immediately find a scapegoat. Not all of our fellow citizens react this way, fortunately. The vast majority are open and tolerant people. We see them during our antiracist demonstrations. We are moved when we see them coming in such numbers and encouraging a movement like ours.

Some people have doubts, and we share their questions during our debates. Every debate that we organize brings together at least four hundred people. We sometimes feel like politicians, since people expect responses and solutions from us. But the questions and doubts that they express most consistently and most often have to do with unemployment. They are afraid of the young people who burn cars, but this fear is amplified by the media, which leads to the impression that this phenomenon exists everywhere—even the urban uprisings were blown out of proportion. When in reality, a journalist who does in-depth research will realize that it's neither structural nor rooted in people's mentality. During the riots in the suburbs last fall, there were daily reports on television as well as in the international press. One would have thought that all of France was in flames even though the riots occurred in only some neighborhoods. It needs to be recognized that the people in the housing projects tried to resist; they went into the streets and shouted at the kids who wanted to make trouble. There was some game playing; for example, some young people used the television coverage to provoke other youths. That was proved when the violence stopped after some of the media outlets grasped the situation and quit televising their reports. It also has to be admitted that the riots were extinguished "thanks" to drug dealers who could no longer do business. All the same, the police, too, did their work well; there were no blunders. This has to be recognized. That was my great fear. Unfortunately, there were the deaths of Zyed and Bouna in the electrical plant, and I hope that the guilty parties are punished.[8] But besides those two children, there was neither murder nor vengeance.

The other immigrant—the immigrant without papers—he doesn't just hug the walls; he creeps, he hides, because he doesn't have papers, and he is a victim of the intensification of police controls. He knows he is in a precarious position, both psychologically and emotionally. Our citizens lump all immigrants together, whether they have papers or not; their vision is blurred. In our collective imaginary, we still see the immigrant as a poor fellow wearing a cap—black or dark-skinned, illiterate—who comes with a swarm of kids seeking a handout.

Sometimes it seems that Le Pen's ideas have succeeded in damaging public opinion. Those ideas have been picked up and reworked by the left as well as the right. Both have made terrible and false declarations. Today, the immigrant must be defined differently: an immigrant is someone who has come to build France, to work, and to make a living. Today, immigration has changed colors. Lately the talk is about the immigration of Eastern Europeans. These people more closely resemble the local Gaulois. They are white, blond, with blue eyes. They look more like the French and thus cause less fear. There is less collective drama in their common history with France than there was for Algeria with the war of independence. There aren't the same frustrations or spirit of revenge as is hidden in our collective memory.

Nonetheless, the duty of memory is necessary if we are going to achieve an intelligent relationship between our peoples, and above all if we are going to avoid having certain ravens or vultures reprise the theme of revenge to set these "ethnic" communities against one another. I think we have to transmit French history to all of our children, just as it existed, even in its most tragic episodes, whether those be decolonization, the Shoah, or, of course, the slave trade, which still doesn't even appear in the history books. This must be done in such a way that the past matters to everyone, that it appears as our collective memory and not as sequential memories in which Maghrebi people will have their memory of the process of colonization and

8. The deaths of Zyed Benna, age fifteen, and Bouna Traoré, age seventeen, triggered the riots that took place in France during late October and early November of 2005. The boys had been playing soccer with a group of friends in a field near their housing project in Clichy-sous-Bois north of Paris. When they encountered a police patrol on their way home, the boys scattered. Zyed, Bouna, and a third boy climbed the fence of an electrical plant to hide, and the two younger boys were accidentally electrocuted inside the plant. In the protests and riots that followed, high unemployment in the projects and police harassment and brutality were the issues most often cited by protesters as contributing factors.

others a memory of the history of enslavement. We currently find ourselves in a situation where memories are juxtaposed [rather than shared], and there is a futile competition over who has suffered the most. I am opposed to this war of memories that provokes discord and uselessly fans the flames. We have to think of these memories as belonging to everyone; they constitute the patrimony of all of our citizens. The suffering of former slaves touches me as much as the suffering of my own ancestors who were colonized, for example. But I am equally touched by the suffering of those who have been deported and by the suffering of those who have seen their families disappear into concentration camps. No one has a monopoly on these tragic moments from our past. It is our collective history. That is why I have always said to my Jewish friends that the Shoah does not belong to them exclusively. The images of the concentration camps haunt my mind and break my heart. And I continue to wonder how we could have let this happen. It is the defeat of reason and of humanity.

We must remain vigilant at every moment to make sure that "never again" becomes a reality for each day and for every one of us.

I am convinced that the struggles for the rights of women and for equality between women and men are the vectors of emancipation for all humanity. This fight today represents the epicenter of the struggle against all forms of obscurantism and fascism.

Integration

Mohammed

A review of the history of migratory flow and immigration in France reveals that it has occurred in two different periods. The first, which lasted until the 1970s, is known as the "period of labor immigration" [*période de l'immigration de main-d'œuvre*]. France needed manual laborers to cope with the growing demands of its national economy and sent out an appeal for immigrants, notably from the former colonies in Africa and the Maghreb, after having previously called for Polish, Spanish, and Portuguese immigrants. The second period ran from the end of the seventies to the end of the eighties, when there was a shift in immigration from temporary manual workers to permanent settlement. It became clear that those who had come here to work were now here to stay. Most of them had gotten married; others brought their wives over in accordance with policies that allowed immigration for family reunification. Those workers began to have children here—children born on French soil; children who knew only France and French schools; children who knew only the French language and French culture. These children are French and consider themselves French on the inside.

It's the small but very French gesture that takes you by surprise, makes you French without your noticing it. Even the uniqueness and traditions kept alive in the heart of family life cannot override this feeling of being French. Public life, life with others, school, clubs, all these make you a French kid.

In the eighties, France was faced with a real integration problem. Suddenly people who had grown up in France were running up against this question of integration and problems caused by discrimination. They were hit with the question "Who are we?" We had never talked about that before; it was unknown territory . . . But people did begin to think about the emergence of this social question and the concentration of poverty, without finding real solutions, however.

Beginning in 1983, local authorities assumed more and more power. Local politicians began to realize that there were problems in every town: tensions between different communities, problems of violence and delinquency. How, given the available resources, were these problems to be handled so as to bring about social peace? It was in this context that the idea was born—an all too easy, mediocre, and stupid idea—of resorting to local figures of patriarchal authority. It was called "the big brother policy." It basically reproduced a structure found back in the countries of origin. It was thought that using "the big brother policy" would bring about social peace. Indeed, during the eighties, there was a semblance of peace that fostered a nascent equilibrium between communities, but only at a very local level. In this way, the seeds of communitarianism were sown in the eighties. From the beginning, the conditions were ripe for communitarianism.

Now, in fact, local politics were incapable of fixing the problems. During those years, local powers were relatively constrained; those of the general council were very limited, like those of cities, and as for regions, they had no powers.[1] The current regional powers came only much later. The Jacobin state remained caught between the desire for a centralized national policy and contradictions that had to be managed at the local level in each town.

These were the elements at the origin of this baseless policy, a policy that gave rise to communitarianism with its first protests in 1989 at the time of the [initial] headscarf affair. This protest was the prelude to what is happening today. Like many of the French, I was one of those who thought that school and blue jeans would prevail over the headscarf. So I signed this general petition that acknowledged the wearing of the headscarf as a cultural rather than religious symbol. I believed it was necessary to let young girls go to school with a headscarf. Today I regret not having seen what was coming. Now it's no longer a question of four hundred or a thousand headscarves, but of a veritable phenomenon. Some people say it's their right and that freedom of choice must be defended, but that's just not the case. Freedom to choose requires that the conditions for choice have been met, but they haven't been in the *quartiers*: unemployment, segregated spaces for men and women, machismo, violence, problems with housing, etcetera. Therefore, we can't speak about the freedom to choose, because the conditions for the exercise of this freedom are lacking.

1. The general council (*conseil général*) is an administrative body within a French *département*. —Trans.

This was the situation we found ourselves in back in 1989, with cases that were the prelude to what would happen in the following years.

Today, because of her position against wearing headscarves at school, Fadela has been able to open up people's thinking on this question. She has enabled a lot of girls to fight back and to express their disagreement with respect to the headscarf question. The law against religious symbols in school is a rallying point for all girls, especially those who are under pressure to wear the headscarf, and also those who already wear it and who will be able to rely on this support later to escape a slow social death. I invite those who have criticized the law in the name of freedom to ponder this sentence from the Abbé Grégoire: "Between the weak and the strong, it is freedom which oppresses the weak and the law which sets them free."

The law against wearing a headscarf at school is an important law, not for the French Republic, which can defend itself, but in the struggle against fascistic obscurantism. The Muslim population has missed an opportunity of the greatest importance. It was a historic opportunity, and it should have been seized as an occasion to seal the pact with the Republic. I believe that the representatives of what one might call "the Muslim community," notably the UOIF, the Union of Islamic Organizations of France [Union des organisations islamiques de France], had a great responsibility. They should have had the presence of mind to say that the public school is sacred and the principle of secularism should be inviolate. Just imagine, if they had only once expressed themselves in this way, we wouldn't be where we are today. But these so-called leaders played one-upmanship; they fought for recognition of the veil and left the rest of the world with a disastrous impression. In the debates that we participated in with Fadela in Arab countries, people thought that Muslims were being chased down in France. They didn't know that the French Constitution is one of the few constitutions that say expressly that "the secular republic knows all religions but recognizes none." In other words, the secular republic treats religions equally. I think, as a matter of fact, that religious questions aren't a priority for the French. The sometimes tragic story of secularism in the eldest daughter of the Church has left indelible traces.[2] Nonetheless, this situation has seemed incomprehensible to many; they've had doubts that the Muslim religion could be integrated into France. They have doubted it all the more as the positions taken by some of the "spokespersons" for the Muslim community, ignorant of the history of the Republic, have made our fellow

2. France is called "the eldest daughter of the Church" because of its long, unbroken association with the Roman Catholic Church, stretching back to the baptism of Clovis in 496 A.D. Clovis was the first to unite all the Franks under one ruler and proclaimed Catholicism the state religion. —Trans.

citizens shudder. For my part, I think that Islam in France, or of France, needs both an Abbé Grégoire and a Victor Hugo.

I think that the struggle over the wearing of the headscarf in school is very important. It's a symbolic struggle that affects the daily, lived experience of human beings. This struggle consists simply in saying to them: "You have the freedom to live freely, but you have to uphold the conditions for the exercise of that freedom." It is a difficult struggle, because it touches on people's most intimate and personal convictions. It affects the young women and girls, thirteen to sixteen years old, who decide to wear a headscarf. What part does the personal play in the path that leads a young girl to keep herself closed up in a veil? What part does suffering play, and what part does secrecy play? It seems to us necessary not to stigmatize, and not to lose sight of what's important, not to judge. In fact, we are at a turning point, where progress has to be demanded and freedom of thought protected. To do this, we have to enter the dialogue, but with firmness.

Discrimination

Fadela

It is clear that today there is even more discrimination and racism directed at the Arab and black populations. I don't say this because I am of Algerian origin. Unfortunately, it's a fact. I observe it every day; it's a reality that every one of us can see. New immigrants aren't the only ones affected. There are also many young members of the second generation who are French and are still subject to discrimination. This is intolerable and must be denounced. It's already intolerable that anyone at all, no matter who they are, has to put up with racism or discrimination, whether they are a woman, disabled, or elderly.

The vast majority of victims of discrimination, however, are French. Prejudice targets a certain population category: Beur and black youth. In this respect, television plays a harmful role: these young men are often portrayed as petty thieves and the kind who burn cars. I understand that some of the French are fearful when they see gangs of young people showing up at demonstrations with their baseball caps worn backward and engaging in violence, as happened last spring. Skin color no longer matters. The mere thought of "backward caps" immediately conjures up an image of a young person from the projects. And then one thinks Arab or black. People forget the young Gaulois, who might also be agents of terrible violence. It's not just the children of immigrants who engage in such activity. The principal source of this violence comes from the concentration of poor people in one place. In no way does this excuse the behavior of those youths who came and smashed up Paris in the demonstrations, hitting and harassing their peers. I strongly condemn them.

I have also observed that the newest immigrants aren't coming from the countries of the Maghreb. And I see a great difference in their integration.

They are more easily accepted and acceptable. There's a lot of work still to be done, but I'm optimistic. With trade and globalization, the entire world is becoming a village, encouraging cross-cultural relationships. Cultural forms are mixing to such an extent that I sometimes feel as if a single universal culture is emerging. I would prefer that each country keep its own specificity, because I find that it contributes to the richness of each individual. Myself, I'm a patchwork; to be sure, I've embraced French culture and claim it as my own, but at the same time I have my own identity because my ancestors were born on the other side. I am of Algerian origin, Kabyle in particular, and I am proud of my Kabyle culture, my oral traditions, my myths, stories, and legends. This enriches me more than it handicaps me. To share my culture with my neighbor François, who in turn tells me his Auvergnate folktales—which, by the way, has happened frequently, since I'm from the Auvergne region—this has always constituted an enrichment, a reciprocity. That's how we come to struggle against prejudices. I have always been convinced that there are very few racists in our country, true racists in the ideological sense of the term. In contrast, when our country or when Europe goes through a difficult period, with globalization and neoliberalism, which have terrible consequences in every country, but especially in the lives of individuals, fear rises and becomes fixed—as is only human—on a scapegoat, who bears the brunt of our anxiety. But for me, this is a question of a historically specific racism that fluctuates with economic difficulties. In France, for example, with the impoverishment of different strata of the working class and the middle classes, the National Front has become the premier party in the housing projects. It remains so today. The extreme right needs to be eradicated by attacking poverty head on. When a family no longer believes in the future, when there's no longer any hope, when there's unemployment, when your children, too, are having trouble finding work, when the bills add up and the end of the month becomes an obstacle course, when you see that a good education for your children is so expensive, it's easy to give in to feelings of envy and spite toward your neighbor just because he is a "foreigner." All of this seems to me more like a process of mental contagion, a series of petty acts of meanness rather than true racism. Bringing the feelings, the resentment, out into the open is enough to calm the situation. I have seen it in specific events we've held, for example, at dinners that have been organized to take place in the heart of the *quartier*—banquets where the whole population participates together—and in which we really see extraordinary things happen: acts of solidarity and conviviality. I don't want to minimize racism and discrimination, which I certainly condemn and denounce, but I truly believe that it is possible to get out of this pettiness. Our political efforts, on the right and the left, need to make all of our fellow citizens feel that they are part of a single republic and feel respected for who they are.

Count me among those who very much regret that the Communist Party is not better-established in our at-risk neighborhoods. I am not a communist, even though I really like the notion—fundamental for communism—of solidarity. I think the party is an essential actor in our country, and it has had an extraordinary impact in that it succeeded in getting whole generations to dream. Hence I regret the diminished influence of the communists in the housing projects, along with other solidarity-building and working-class education networks. I come from a generation that benefited from such things and remember them from when I was a little girl. It was part of a certain tradition of working-class education, and I immersed myself in it when I was a kid. That tradition helped me become the citizen I am today and helped me want to be an active citizen. They took us on; there was a mix of kids from the neighborhood. Every Thursday there were activities: we would participate in different things, different activities, surrounded by adults who shared their values with us and didn't judge the little Arab kids they were taking care of. On the contrary, they treated us with a certain respect. We had the sense of being recognized and liked, just the same as the kids named François or Christiane. There was a feeling of solidarity among us. This experience helped me become who I am, and at the same time it kept me from developing prejudices about other people. My father and mother taught me tolerance and never to give in to ideas that could reject the other because of his identity. My father was subjected to racism and never wanted us to be subjected to it or to subject others to it. We were aware of our condition, of belonging to the working class. We knew that we were the children of immigrants and that the future would be twice as difficult for us as for others because of our situation and our condition. Today the communists have been replaced, either by fascists on the extreme right—support for Le Pen is growing rapidly—or by the Islamists, the obscurantists on every side, who have gained ground by promoting values that make it impossible to live together in mutual respect. They advocate hate speech that targets women, but also others, those who welcome us, whites, Jews. We have to combat this constant discourse of rejection, while remaining clear-headed. It must be possible to fight against Islamist fascism—a political hijacking of the Muslim religion that has caused much harm—in the same way that society previously fought against white fascism. The communists still play a central role in this struggle and remain active in certain housing projects, such as those in Saint-Denis, where important initiatives continue to forge social bonds.

We are paying a high cost for the loss of communist influence and a network of solidarity-building associations in the projects. No self-respecting immigrant can vote for Le Pen. And yet, what makes me very afraid is that this is just what some children of immigrants have done. Unfortunately, we have firsthand accounts: some children of immigrant parents voted for the extreme right. It pains me to see that people who look like me could bring themselves to vote for a party that is fascist, racist, and antisemitic. It seems incomprehensible, as if it were some sort of suicidal amnesia, the opposite of a collective memory. It's as if they have forgotten that our mothers and fathers were immigrants. These youths who voted extreme right, even if they're still in the minority, are a source of concern. They forget that they're voting for a political program that seeks to eliminate the existence of immigrants, and thus of their father and their mother. They justify themselves by calling on selective memory, because according to their logic, what they're doing is participating in the extreme right's fight against the Jews. For me, they are dangerous. They vote extreme right. They're the enemy; it doesn't matter that they are named Mohamed. It is no longer my problem, it is theirs. It is vital and necessary to denounce the collusion between the lines advanced by the extreme right, notably antisemitism, and the theses of the Islamists, which come together and congeal. This is a grave danger.

There are two ways to resist this danger. The first solution is individual: we need to call upon the responsibility of each one of us as a citizen. We have to be able to say that we do not accept a certain set of behaviors that damage the values of our country. We have to retain our capacity to revolt, but to revolt in a positive and constructive way that does not endanger foreigners but guarantees liberty and equality for all. The other solution is collective and political in substance, in the sense that we are all members of the same community: we need to call upon politicians and make them do their job. Their job is to forbid zones of relegation in our country. We have to ask them to stop concentrating immigrants and populations descended from immigrants [in the ghettos]. The creation of these no-man's-lands where the poor among us live—or rather, merely survive—has to be stopped. We need to build virtual frontiers where struggling and impoverished populations can live together in the same space with middle-class populations. And all should benefit from the same public schools, whose mission is to aid in the formation of future citizens. Today, the opposite happens: certain populations are set apart from the rest of France. This struggle began with the slogan "End the ghettos," which was taken up and acted on by politicians on the left and the right. This initiative began under Mitterrand, with Roland Castro and his project "Banlieues 89."[1] It continues today with a few more resources. But what I find regrettable about the current government is that while it has testified to a willingness to do more in at-risk neighborhoods and to try to rehabilitate them with the tools of urban renewal, the human is never fully taken into account, despite the intentions of Jean-Louis Borloo.[2] Cooperating with those who live there, in a real and concrete way, is not accorded enough importance. We need real follow-through and a return to grassroots, not just grand words and speeches that get swept up in the Republic's whims. When we speak of fighting unemployment, we need tangible means, government administrators authorized to establish ways to evaluate whether the policies put in place are relevant and effective—without waiting ten years only to realize that the government has made mistakes. It would be better to work more modestly and on a tighter schedule. Every year or two, you should look at the results of unemployment policies: observe them, modify them, improve them. You should get down to the everyday level, assess the situation, and resist making grand pronouncements about new directions according to the whims of some political calendar. We have plenty of brainpower, but so much of it has so lost touch with reality that it just turns in circles. These brainiacs forget to defend the people at the bottom. The elite of the ENA (the École nationale d'administration) are completely off base; they don't see what's happening or how things work in the housing projects. But that doesn't stop them from saying what they think needs to be done. I have almost never seen anyone from the ENA come into the projects, either in normal times or during the riots, with the exception of the prefect who came when the situation exploded. Outside of emergency situations, never! We need real encounters and a capacity for self-criticism. I'm not interested in those who propose that everything be torn down and rebuilt from scratch; on the contrary, I'm interested in imagining concrete solutions based on relevant ideas. Criticism also involves observation, and I see that in certain quarters, notably in at-risk neighborhoods, in spite of everything that has been done in the last thirty years, things continue to go badly and even get worse. I think that the brains behind public administration need to set aside their codes and their particular analytical frameworks in order to hear people directly and to see how to adjust their aim, looking always to the benefit and well-being of humanity.

1. Banlieues 89 was a design-led initiative in French urban policy aimed at fighting social exclusion by challenging current practices in the design of both inner-city and suburban spaces and building projects. —Trans.

2. Borloo was the minister in charge of urban renewal from 2002 to 2004. —Trans.

Equality

Fadela

There's a big difference between at-risk neighborhoods and those that are completely closed off. At-risk neighborhoods are neighborhoods where there's a little delinquency, where the unemployment rate is significant, but where there's still ethnic diversity. There's still life in at-risk neighborhoods; there are public services, and the inhabitants and regional administrations still want to maintain links with the city center. By contrast, in those neighborhoods that are completely closed off, life is catastrophic. There are no public services anymore, no associations; people live in scandalous housing accommodations. Whole populations of the same ethnic group are concentrated in a single set of buildings. To see destitution, there's no need to go to Africa; deeply impoverished neighborhoods can be found on the outskirts of Paris. I visited the Bosquets housing project in 1993, Grigny in 1991, and each time I was devastated to see the conditions people were living in: the mailboxes are broken, gang tags are everywhere, it's dirty, there's no longer even a caretaker. Everything is dilapidated; destitution seeps from every pore, and rubs off on those who live there. The inhabitants seem defeatist and fatalistic, even those who are lucky enough to have a job. The mayors and the state have completely abandoned these neighborhoods; no bus dares to serve these areas at night. No one has the will to open these neighborhoods back up. The only reason these ghettos exist is that a process was set in motion and allowed to run its course, all the way to its horrifying conclusion. Our nation and our politicians should be ashamed. In a city, all neighborhoods can and should be connected to the city center. We need to oversee a redistribution of public transportation and public services to breathe life back into these areas. One such neighborhood in Argenteuil is the size of an entire city. This requires maintaining basic public services. At some point, the state must guarantee everyone access to public services. Things need to be arranged so there's as little decline as possible. This responsibility is incumbent upon politicians. There aren't just young kids named Mohamed and Mamadou in these neighborhoods; there is also little Benoît. And when Mohamed and Mamadou engage in acts of violence, they need to be punished. But I would rather see politicians get them off these reservations where the poor are parked before they become capable of such asinine behavior. Their right to live with dignity has to be guaranteed.

As for violence and delinquency, I agree first and foremost that everything possible needs to be done to stop recidivism. But we have to know how to draw a distinction. When it's the first time that someone has acted up, that has to be taken into consideration. We need to teach the kid a lesson, and this has to be done right away. The sense of impunity arises when too much time elapses between the discovery of the act, the judgment, and the application of a sanction. I remain committed to the work done by the justice system—despite its lack of finances—and admire what some judges are doing, such as the children's judges at Bobigny. I share the position of Mr. Rosenczveig, the president of the tribunal that oversees children's cases at Bobigny, who has said that the prevention of delinquency in minors does not depend only on the justice system. I would add that neither does it depend on the severity of the punishment. Thinking that it does makes us feel better, but it doesn't solve the problem. Other factors are in play.

Certainly, we need to destroy that sense of impunity that some juvenile delinquents feel. That will happen if there's the political will to give our justice system the human and financial resources it needs to do its work dispassionately and without demagoguery.

But it will also happen by breaking down the process that leads to delinquency, genuinely attacking its causes. They're well-known. We have to act; these are our children who are in danger and who put others in danger. If we—parents, social agents, educators, and above all elected representatives—if we do not assume our responsibilities, we are not doing our job. I remain convinced that judgment has to be balanced between prevention and punishment. But the violence won't decrease in the housing projects unless the means for prevention are increased. This means that we have to increase the number of teachers; we have to establish new policies based on neighborhood organizations [*une politique associative*]; we need to expand the number of people who are active links in the network. There are fewer and fewer teachers, and it is difficult to convince the authorities to increase the number of community centers. Our community center is very recent, and we had to fight for it.[1] It works well because people—children, mothers, fathers—have made it their own. Sometimes the older folks are a little annoyed and say that it is mainly young people who benefit from the center. Community centers serve a real social function when they are run correctly. But the responsibility for this doesn't fall only on those who run the centers directly; it's also the responsibility of those who determine the budget lines: the finances and the personnel are both necessary. We have denounced the lack of oversight in the management of community centers. When activities are proposed, it's necessary to take responsibility for them, and also to ensure that both boys and girls are welcome. It's a question not only of money, but also of will. Some people in the housing projects have terrorized youth workers in order to get rid of the girls; and the girls have given in because they don't have a choice.

The idea is to fight for mixed social spaces [*la mixité*] and never to capitulate: youth workers and program leaders must make sure that *mixité* is respected. It's a question of a power struggle. In every Ni Putes Ni Soumises activity, boys and girls participate together. If even a single boy protests, I will explain to him in private in my office, for four hours if necessary, how important it is to be together with the girls, since society is mixed. And generally I manage to convince him . . . But we always have to remain willing to go through these explanations and to resist power struggles, also with mothers. Often it's the mothers who transmit archaic traditions according to which girls are not the equal of boys. In order to win this battle, we have to address these women's experience, because it quickly becomes apparent that they have always found themselves in a submissive role. At home they're queens, they're the backbone of the family, they have complete control over their domestic time and space, because the husband is often absent. They decide everything, but still under the husband's control. If one of the children fails in some way, the mothers are held responsible, and the whole family turns on them. When you begin to dissect what they say about the transmission of values, about the pride and honor of the family resting on the shoulders of women, the mothers begin to speak about themselves. At bottom, there is this feeling of revolt that has long been smothered. When they first come in contact with our organization, other than their shock at the name Ni Putes Ni Soumises, they end up telling me that if they were twenty years old, they would join us.

1. The Paris headquarters of Ni Putes Ni Soumises are lodged in a community center they have named La maison de la mixité. The center provides free social services including counseling and legal advice, offers weekly educational and social programs, and serves as a drop-in and resource center for women and children. It is located in the 20th arrondissement in Paris. —Trans.

We are winning some battles. When these women come to encourage us, it warms our hearts. Little by little, they attempt to shed their old habits, to change, to speak to their son in the same way they speak to their daughter, to give the boys some domestic chores. And the boys oppose their mothers, because they don't want to lose their privileged status.

The situation in the *quartiers* is very complex and very diverse. There's not only the struggle against sexism and male chauvinism, there's also the struggle against the Islamists, who oppose all Western values. They have demonized the West, proclaiming that Western values are those of the devil. These Islamists and their supporters feed the unfortunate idea of a "clash of civilizations." For my part, I totally refute this thesis; in contrast, I believe in a great chain of solidarity between civilizations. For me, the West is the bearer of Enlightenment values: the values of liberty, equality, and progress. These values affect all of humanity.

When certain Islamists come along and say that these are Western values, I tell them that these are the values of the whole world, the values of good sense, and that good sense can be universalized. For them, women's freedom is restricted to the right to have children and to stay at home; anything beyond that is debauchery. This is also the view of women who wear the veil; they adhere to the same discourse.

Of course, we aren't the only association to take this line; there are a dozen others in the projects. Nevertheless, we helped to break the code of silence. Today we have to work to create a dynamic that brings together all those who strive daily to live with others within the framework of French republican values.

Some sociologists and intellectuals have said that the impact of Ni Putes Ni Soumises can't be measured yet and that it won't be known until ten years from now. The signs that show us that we are moving forward and making progress are first of all the general awareness, and then the improved dialogue between parents and children, and at the same time between boys and girls, and even between brothers and sisters.

There are more debates about equality between the sexes, about women having control over their own bodies, something that seems difficult for girls to manage and that makes the boys afraid. Ni Putes Ni Soumises has been hotly debated within families, and also at mosques. In the mosques, despite what one might imagine and beyond the shock caused by the slogan, some spokesmen for Islam in France support us: the rector of the Mosque of Paris, Dalil Boubakeur; Soheib and Ghaleb Bencheikh; Béthoul Fekkar-Lamiotte, who was the first woman to have a seat on the French Council of the Muslim Faith [Conseil français du culte musulman]; and many others.

The only ones who oppose our struggle belong—surprise, surprise—to the Islamist movement.

In French families, there is also work to do. Little Benoît says the same things as little Mohamed and has the same demands: that a girl has to be a virgin before marriage to uphold the family's honor. This creates all kinds of difficulties for little Christiane in this family, who has watched her mother take part in feminist debates and today sees her brother impose his reactionary ideas on her. Our association tries to play a role in this struggle, but we've only just begun; we have a long way to go.

Laws of the Projects

FADELA: One of the objectives of Ni Putes Ni Soumises was to liberate speech. When we break the silence, we help so many young girls put words to their suffering. One young girl is now talking openly about the gang rape she suffered in 1999 over the course of several months. She decided to speak up and blow the whistle. A series of arrests followed, and there was a stir in her neighborhood. Some of the boys were quickly released because they were not implicated in the investigation. What is proving to be really difficult for the young woman is that she is getting pressure from all sides: from her own family, from her brother. She is being denigrated: people are saying that she's sick, that she should go to a psychiatric hospital. All kinds of things are being done to discredit her testimony so that she will keep quiet and take back everything she has said. On the one hand, some of the boys in the neighborhood, her family, and her brother are to blame, but also, and this worries us much more, her immediate social circle is at fault: her so-called best friends. These girls say that she has a bad reputation, and that she spoke out about this gang rape to vindicate herself. Despite the fight that Ni Putes Ni Soumises is leading, despite the outcry we have raised, and despite the support of other organizations in her neighborhood, her fight remains painful and isolated. Everything remains very difficult. The laws of the ghetto are still there, all too present; we are a long way from the values of the Republic in this neighborhood. But we are clear-headed. We have created this movement thanks to public opinion. We know that we have work to do, that it's going to be a long, drawn-out process. The question is, how are we going to win the battle? We are fighting for respect for women, for equality, and so that all the crimes committed against women will be solved. The pressure still exists, but we have to continue; we cannot give in. Some, like this young girl, pay a high price. Her mother strongly defended her and encouraged her to press charges. But now this girl doesn't see her mother anymore, because conditions were so intolerable that she had to leave the projects. They keep in touch by telephone. But it's really hard for her.

In the *quartiers*, the girls are beginning to speak up. Nevertheless, whenever a situation arises, as soon as anything is known, a rumor always starts, something about the girl's reputation. People say that she's easy, that she screws all the guys in the neighborhood, that she's a whore. Some boys behave offensively toward girls in this type of situation. Gang rapes don't happen just in the housing projects; they are happening more and more in all our *quartiers*. I don't like it when the word "*tournante*" is used in talking about the rapes these girls suffer, because it strips the crime of its severity.[1] "*Tournante*" refers to something like a joint: you pass the joint around, you "pass" the girl around. That's where the term comes from. It's a nice word, even a playful one. The very use of it is a sign that some young men aren't even conscious of the severity of their actions. Whenever you say "*tournante*," young people laugh; on the other hand, as soon as you say "rape," they start to feel fear. Words have a meaning, and their meaning must be reclaimed. We know from the rumors that gang rapes exist. For the girls who are subjected to them, the rapes are not recognized; they don't take on an existence until the moment when the girls are able to go press charges at the police station. As soon as they have the courage to speak up, to break the code of silence, mentally and physically, something happens. Very often, in fact, we're called on by girls who have decided to act. We go with them to press charges; we give them psychological and legal support. Either they have already pressed charges and are calling for our support, or they are looking for someone to listen, to help, to provide assistance. They know they have no moral judgment to fear from us and that they will be taken seriously. They will not be criticized as stigmatizing the projects, boys, Arabs, or blacks. Most often they call on us after having pressed charges. Many continue to maintain their silence for fear of retaliation from the housing project, from the neighborhood, from the social community. When a girl is going to speak out, she is considered a snitch. From the moment she decides to say what happened, she is said to be cooking something up with the police. The girl and her family pay a high price. What a way to prevent someone from taking action! The girls will fight back only when they have suffered too much and when they have too much rage. They know that they can go press charges. However, they often prefer to suffer in silence rather than make their family suffer. They're ashamed to have their parents and family know they've been raped. So in most cases they keep quiet, at the risk of killing themselves psychologically. I know of situations in which girls have been totally destroyed. They close themselves off, don't say anything, shut down, stop communicating with the

1. *Tournante* is an adjectival form used to describe something that rotates or turns, as in a rotating presidency or a revolving door. —Trans.

outside world. They create their own private world. Sometimes when we do interventions in schools, students come to us, in secret, to tell us that one of the girls in their class is acting strangely. Then we help break the silence, and in some cases they open up, sometimes so much that they start to talk in front of everyone and to speak out. Occasionally the principal is angry because he fears for the reputation of his school. But in most cases he turns out to be wonderful and helps us quite a bit, with real follow-up, mentoring, and contact with the young girl's parents.

MOHAMMED: I am seeing an increase in awareness. The girls from the *quartiers* are refusing to be pushed around. The fight remains difficult, because there is strong resistance from the boys' side. What struck me in the Fontenay-sous-Bois affair was the reaction of some of the boys' lawyers, who spoke of a "suburban Dutroux affair."[2] The arrests following the allegation were important, almost sensational; more than thirty people were summoned for questioning. The girl provided names, and the testimony of others made it possible to follow up on leads and find the guilty parties. Some have been taken into custody. Others have been detained for questioning. For the moment, we don't know which parts of this affair are true, false, or exaggerated. The work of the police and the justice system will clarify that for us. But this affair reveals that there is more awareness now about violence against women. The struggle against this form of violence has become an important issue worldwide: in Germany, Holland, Belgium, Morocco, among others. The United Arab Emirates organized a conference in 2005 against gender violence in the Arab world—that was a first! It's often thanks to the courage

2. "The Fontenay-sous-Bois affair" is a reference to the case Amara speaks of at the beginning of this essay. "A 'suburban Dutroux affair" is a reference to the so-called "Dutroux scandal" in Belgium in 1996, during the course of which the Belgian judicial system came under severe public attack. Marc Dutroux is a Belgian who was convicted of having kidnapped, tortured, and sexually abused six girls ranging in age from eight to nineteen, four of whom he murdered. The public was outraged to learn that he had been released from prison in 1992 after serving only three years of a thirteen-year sentence for raping several other young girls. Also disturbing was the information that the police had been present at Dutroux's house while the girls were being held there, and even more damaging was that the police had failed to act even though they were informed in 1993 that Dutroux was building cells in his home allegedly to hold girls before sending them overseas. The judicial crisis was exacerbated in October 1996 when Belgium's highest court removed the investigating magistrate from the case for violating his duty under Belgian law to remain strictly neutral. The magistrate had attended a fundraising dinner for the parents of the victims. His removal sparked massive public demonstrations, with 250,000 to 300,000 people marching in protest in front of the Palais de Justice in Brussels. These events led the government to propose numerous constitutional reforms to the justice system. United Nations Commission on Human Rights, "Interim Report on the Mission of the Special Rapporteur to Belgium." —Trans.

and determination of women that we are called upon and shaken out of our guilty silence.

Rania al-Baz, a young newscaster on a Saudi television channel, is a good example. Disfigured by her husband in 2003, she refused to adhere to the code of silence or feel guilty. Armed with her courage, she exposed to the entire world what the majority of women in her country are at risk of suffering. She recounts her story in a poignant book that was published in France.[3] She became a Ni Putes Ni Soumises activist and a spokesperson for our movement in the Middle East. After a brief stay in France, she left to work at a television station in Beirut. Saudi society will someday salute her courage and lucidity, which have already helped to lay a path there that will lead to rights for all women. Rania al-Baz is our friend, our sister, our partner in struggle. Everywhere in the world, women are on the front lines of the fight for emancipation and equality. Everywhere they are saying no to violence. In France the fight exists, but sometimes it is paradoxical and even strange, especially when one observes that certain feminists consider wearing the veil an expression of liberty, even a vehicle for emancipation. The ambivalent attitude of certain feminist organizations has contributed to legitimizing the discourse of the "*indigènes de la République*," which is at the forefront of the discourse of victimization.[4]

There are some girls who recognize themselves in the *indigènes de la République* and who prefer to interiorize the violence they experience rather than to demand that someone pay. Our work is to be respectful and to say to these girls from the *quartiers*: "You can express yourselves. You can defend your ideas. And this path will lead you to liberty."

We also see it on other levels, for example, on that of the Muslim *intégristes.* Those obscurantist ideas are seductive. It has nothing to do with spirituality, which has to be defended and guaranteed. What is happening in our neighborhoods can be observed everywhere: Egypt, Algeria, Pakistan, in developing countries. We also see it in Europe with the World Cup: there's this huge organization of mass prostitution near the stadiums, which elicits

3. Rania al-Baz, *Défigurée* (Paris: Michel Laffont, 2006). (Author's Note)

4. The "Appeal by the Indigenous Peoples of the Republic for the Upholding of Anticolonial Laws" (L'appel des indigènes de la République pour la tenue d'assises de l'anticolonialisme) was issued in January 2005 on several websites. The petition denounced the racism of postcolonial French society, but did so in language that many viewed as unnecessarily inflammatory and as pitting the "indigenous" population against the "French," as if there were no overlap between these communities and no differences within each side. Several thousand people signed the manifesto, although some prominent signers withdrew their names after Tariq Ramadan added his signature. Ramadan is a leading figure among intellectual Muslims in the West. He is an Oxford professor and the grandson of the founder of the Muslim Brotherhood, which is committed to establishing a radical form of Islam in Europe. —Trans.

only occasional reactions, as if all of that were a normal, everyday thing . . . We are at a crossroads. If we want to live freely, if we want to make progress, we're going to have to continue to mobilize ourselves. The fight for women's emancipation, if it is powerful, will be capable of overcoming obscurantism and regression. For our part, in order to counteract this wave of obscurantism, we are trying to put programs in place aimed at increasing awareness and solidarity. We are also trying to develop partnerships with organizations that work for emancipation and gender equality in other countries. For example, we actively support the CSSF, an organization that supports the education of young girls in the rural areas of Morocco.[5] Basically, in some villages there are many families who cannot afford to finance the girls' transition from primary to middle school. It is often at this age that a girl's destiny becomes uncertain. She might be subjected to a forced marriage, she might become a maid, or she might simply be forgotten altogether. Fadela organized a visit in May with the support of an excellent magazine, *Femmes du Maroc*, which is spearheading the fight for emancipation and equality. In the company of a delegation of prominent French figures, she went to the south of Morocco to visit some of the first boarding schools constructed there [by the CSSF].

Today we are increasing our fundraising initiatives in order to help this project along.

FADELA: Our young people don't feel like they truly belong to the nation. Having lived so long in a culture of failure, they have developed their own habits of failure and exclusion. This feeling even touches those who have graduated high school and gone on to college, and are in their second or third year of study. Discrimination has wreaked havoc in these young people's heads. It has created a mental ghetto where nothing is cultivated except the strategy of failure and fatalism. Instead of examining their own lives, fighting back, and doing something to become actors in their own lives, even if it's difficult—we know as well as anyone that it's hard for people who live in at-risk neighborhoods to get out and that it's really a journey—most youth stay within a mentality, a posture, of victimization. And from there they can justify anything and everything. If I'm in a certain situation, it's because of other people. If I'm discriminated against, it's because everyone is racist. If I'm stigmatized, it's because I'm Arab or black. This even goes for little Benoît, because he mimics and reproduces codes of behavior from his housing project and his friends.[6] He may adopt a sexist demeanor toward his own sister, who herself has a mother who participated in the feminist struggle. We are dealing with paradoxical and contradictory behaviors. This is ghetto culture.

5. The CSSF is the Comité de soutien à la scolarisation des filles rurales (Support Committee for the Education of Rural Girls). —Trans.

6. In other words, this victim mentality is found equally among white French youth living in the ghettos. —Trans.

In my opinion, these neighborhoods have been poorly managed for decades, and the magnitude of the situation has never been measured. What are we doing so that blacks, whites, and Beurs can imagine a future? What programs can we put in place to help free them from this logic of failure and victimization? So that they finally feel like full-fledged citizens and realize that the use of violence, as a way of claiming their rights, is not acceptable?

Some people possess the will to fight for universal values and a life together. But others are looking to solidify their ideology and to politically exploit certain categories of the population. They create a politics that generates exclusion and leads toward hatred of the other, toward the crumbling of the national community. This is a great danger, and one of the struggles that Ni Putes Ni Soumises leads is to prevent the propagation of this ideology.

When a young woman reports that she has been the victim of a gang rape, we hope first of all that she will get the psychological and moral relief she needs to enable her to live something like a normal life, but we also hope that the aggressors will comprehend the barbarity of their act. We work to make them aware of the atrocity they have committed, and we inform all the residents of the neighborhood; we do this to break the hold of a certain mentality of solidarity among those boys who take a negative view of our actions. When you make a mistake, you have to pay for it. When someone commits such a horrible crime, it's normal to go before the justice system. We have to stop concealing the truth behind imprecise words that allow the guilty to pass themselves off as victims. On one side we have the victims, who suffer, who have been miserable; on the other side are those who are guilty. But this is not the rule in the housing projects right now. The silent majority are being terrorized by the minority, who want to continue ruling their dominion with complete impunity. Ni Putes Ni Soumises' struggle, then, is to invert the tendency: to turn this silent majority into an active, vocal majority. Some housing projects are subject to a reign of terror by a few boys, obscurantists, radical evangelists [*évangélistes intégristes*], who advocate ideas such as that a woman should stay home, take care of the children, and be closed in so as to avoid any kind of emancipation.

MOHAMMED: In order to invert the power relationship between the silent majority and an active minority, we must not give in to pressure. When Fadela takes strong and clear positions, people say that she stigmatizes Arabs and Muslims. Thus, these people render themselves complicit with what is going on in these neighborhoods: horror, violence, the situation of regression in which many people, often the weakest, find themselves.

Let's go back to the story of Fontenay-sous-Bois, where the justice system is in the process of doing its job because there was an act, a fact. This woman, now a legal adult, comes to see the police and tells them: "I was a victim of multiple rapes, and it went on for years. It happened in this place and that place, with this person and that one." Should the police be passive or should they do their job? Personally, I know the limits of the police and the justice system's reach. I prefer to run the risk of a mistake or an exaggeration rather than to accept the possibility that a rape will go unpunished. When I hear people saying that we stigmatize those whom we should leave alone because the events happened a long time ago, I say that these people are making themselves complicit with the situation of social vulnerability in which the victims, men and women, find themselves. We must not give in, and if a French citizen, or someone who lives in France, is guilty of rape, he must know that he has disfigured someone forever. Raping someone is not like running a red light. To assault a woman is not to be guilty of a misdemeanor like any other. No, it's an unacceptable offense! The wound remains wide open, always present and alive. We are not condemning anyone, but there are no extenuating circumstances. There is a time for the work of the police and the justice system, and there is a time for the work of a citizen.

This latter work must be a pedagogical effort, at a deep level, every day, and in the public interest, not an effort to stigmatize. Some people, who pride themselves on their sociological expertise with I don't know what kind of qualifications, come to tell us that our position is a dangerous one because the frequency of rape has barely increased! But today, in the name of the French Republic and of democracy, we must not accept even a 0.0001 percent increase. Otherwise our struggle makes no sense. If there is even a single woman in the world who is a victim of rape, well, we must fight in the name of that woman. It must be explained to boys that when they rape a girl, that girl might be someone's cousin, someone's girlfriend, or someone's sister. She is a part of him.

At every level of French society, whatever their ethnic origin, people are fed up with violence. They don't hate immigrants or Arabs: they hate violence. That's why they make strong demands about a variety of things, but at the same time they are capable of huge waves of solidarity and generosity, as is evidenced by the support for children who are threatened with being expelled from French schools. In a village near Strasbourg, for example, where an unusually high proportion of people vote for the National Front Party, almost the entire village mobilized in order to save these children. That is France. Those are the gestures that we must recognize. We must look into this duality, because it carries hope. I wage this struggle without second thoughts, without hesitation, with serenity, and I wage it as an Arab Muslim, coming from an immigrant background and living in the *banlieues*.

FADELA: It's this France that we love, this France that rises up against injustice. I find these gestures on the part of anonymous citizens so strong and beautiful; they are participating in an upsurge of solidarity, and it's a profound gesture. It's extraordinary. Public opinion reflects a great fear of crime and violence. This creates an anxiety-prone society that at any given moment can become more radical in its behavior as well as its discourse. And in the end, inevitably, it finds a scapegoat. Often it's the foreigner who is unlike us. One idea joins forces with another to create an amalgam that ends in exclusion, or worse. But when we see these waves of solidarity, people supporting the children in our French public schools who are the children of illegal immigrants, we remain hopeful.

This is the France we are defending and the France of which Ni Putes Ni Soumises is a part. We recognize ourselves in this France. It is for this France, and against antisemitic, xenophobic, and racist discourse, that we fight—to keep this France that we love alive. And we do it even though we are denounced in some quarters by people who claim to have conducted sociological studies. They treat us like anthropological curiosities. I would like for these people to put down their Mont-Blanc pens and come see what really happens in the housing projects. I would like for them to come and explain to me why liberty and equality are not for everyone. How can these people tell me, the daughter of immigrants, who lives in the housing projects, who is a member of the poorest social class, who is working hard, trying to fight—how can they tell me to shut up, to go back to the projects and my mental ghetto? At the risk of being insulted and pointed at, of being accused of paying allegiance to the dominant class, and of joining the chorus of repressive discourse. I pity them, but I certainly wouldn't like to be in their place when they take stock of their lives. One must never be complicit with the forms of oppression by silencing oneself.

What is social order when some of us live in chaos? When we live with the consequences of chaos, and of everything that prevents a person from having all the means to defend herself and to be a true citizen?

MOHAMMED: When Fadela said that parity for young girls in working-class neighborhoods is like a sale at Hermès, she uttered the phrase spontaneously; it came from deep in her gut. She summed up the entire situation. Some French feminists have never forgiven her for that remark. For the last fifteen years, feminism has focused on this question of parity. Certainly it's an essential demand, but it does not capture or resolve all women's problems, especially those who live in underprivileged neighborhoods. A sale at Hermès, it's an opportunity but not for every budget.

FADELA: In the *quartiers*, there's an existing social order. There's an established mode of operation that is very clear to everybody. Ni Putes Ni Soumises aims to undo this social order. We are exploding the established order of things. The housing projects' norms are accepted by certain intellectuals, who don't want us to disturb their theses and who refuse to see the growing power of a few political figures and obscurantists on all sides. Ni Putes Ni Soumises is revolutionary, in the sense that we're striking against the established social norms in our neighborhoods, that is to say, against the oppression of women, against the oppression of individuals. I intend to contribute to the disturbance of the social order that these people want to retain. I'm saying it: I will remain revolutionary if it's necessary. This established social order in the *quartiers*, I don't want it. I yearn for a society in which women in the housing projects live like the women in more well-to-do neighborhoods, where the young people of the projects—whom no one in Parliament represents—can live normally and properly, just like any other young person. If this displeases a few intellectuals who don't find our movement in accordance with their own definition of social order, well, personally, I say: I, too, belong to the legacy of May 1968. Yes, we are against the established order: we want the emancipation of individuals, particularly the poorest among them. There is no reason for the men and women in at-risk neighborhoods, especially the girls of the housing projects, to live in a state of oppression under the pretext that a movement such as ours disturbs the established order in the ghettos and displeases a few intellectuals. It's fashionable to say that the poor are oppressed, but no one dares to say that the oppressed can become active oppressors themselves, because they are oppressed by the system in place, and are themselves in a situation of exclusion. Now, exclusion in no way justifies indirect oppression of the most fragile populations, in this case girls and women. If it's necessary to engage in a pacifist revolution in order to break down the established order in the *quartiers*, I will continue my battle. I will continue to resist.

I think the police and the judicial system have important roles. I count myself among those who believe that, no matter where a person comes from or what someone's background is, each of us has a right to safety. I think that the police should be representative [of the population at large] and should maintain safety in every neighborhood. I only regret that there are behaviors within the French police force that make it seem doubtful whether they can fulfill this mission. Certain police officers should be helped, and others, those who exhibit extremist behaviors, should be pointed out and censured. I know very well that not all police officers are like that. Whenever there's a brawl or a conflict breaks out, we're happy to see the police arrive so that all citizens can live peacefully and get up the next morning to go to work without bags under their eyes or marks on their faces.

In our country, we don't give the judicial system the human and financial resources to act. It made me very uneasy to see, in the trial at Outreau, that the legal system in our country lacked the resources to be properly implemented.[7] There is always the risk of error, because the law is applied

7. In 2004, in the northern town of Outreau, near Boulogne, eighteen suspects were put on trial charged with sexual abuse of children. Seven of the defendants, who had spent up to three years in prison awaiting trial while their children were in foster care, were cleared of all wrongdoing. Six others, including a priest, were convicted despite the collapse of all credible evidence against them. Two couples who admitted abusing their own and each other's children in adjoining flats in public housing in Outreau were given lengthy jail sentences. False accusations made by one of those four, Myriam Delay, as well as by some of the children involved in the case, led investigators to believe that the

by human beings, but in this case the errors were terrible and resulted in the breakup of families and the destruction of human beings. Justice is the sign that we live in a state of law and in a democracy.[8] I regret that today we don't give our legal system what it needs to function and fulfill its beautiful mission. In the housing projects, people often think that justice is for the middle classes, and they are often highly critical of it. When a kid from the ghetto does something stupid, he should be punished immediately so that he won't do it again. Justice has to act the very first time in order to impede and prevent a second offense. Unfortunately, that isn't the case today. I think that when justice is meted out, there is a different set of weights or measures used for cases involving youth from the ghettos. There is unequal treatment according to social class. When it affects those from the favored classes, there are more cases of suspended sentences. I attribute this to the fact that the legal system lacks the human and financial resources that are needed for it to be applied justly. This sentiment is shared by people in the ghettos.

MOHAMMED: The French people need to be made aware that something in the state judicial system isn't working right; they need to be made aware of the limits of this system, which has lost its touch because of inadequate resources, and also because it lacks independence. Even though it may slip up, independence is vital to the justice system. The budget for the judicial system has hardly changed since the nineteenth century. France is not the European country that devotes the most money to its judicial system. Today the question for French society is that of its weakest and most impoverished people. They are often victims of injustice. The police are one thing, the judicial system is another. For me, the judicial system is the place where the two poles of the social contract can ultimately be welded together. Whatever the act, no matter whether someone is the victim or the aggressor, that person must be made to feel that he or she is a citizen. The trial is the crucial moment. Everything is decided there, the possibility of a repeat offense or of comprehending that a wrong has been committed. The judicial system is not only a machine made to punish, it is also a step toward reparation and education.

There is not a logic of repression on one side and a logic of prevention on the other. There is only one logic: that of the general interest. To live together in harmony and the interest of all. To do this, it is necessary to

---

couples were part of an international child-sex ring, which resulted in the other arrests. The magistrate who investigated the case was quite junior and lacked the proper oversight because of severe financial and manpower shortages in the judicial system. —Trans.

8. "State of law" (*État de droit*) is a technical term in French public law denoting a state that operates by means of law and that is itself bound by its own laws. It is a direct translation of the German *Rechtsstaat* and became influential in the French context during the Third Republic (1870–1940). —Trans.

give our judicial system a genuine penal policy that is consistent and harmonious, rather than one that responds to circumstantial and short-term considerations. Punishing in order to prevent recidivism is not the same as punishing in order to show that one has a heavy hand or can be severe.

I think we must fight so that the judicial system can be more independent [of politics] and so that it no longer favors one class over another. It's a fact, as everyone knows, that a poor person and a rich person don't have the same chances, because the legal system also has a technical side, a juridical technique. How many people in France today find themselves going straight to prison when they would have been able to avoid it if they'd had the material resources to take their case to the Court of Cassation?[9] How many people would have been released if they'd had the means to appeal? How many poor people have the opportunity to appeal to the Court of Cassation, which everyone knows is expensive? The question of giving the poor the means to defend themselves in court is an essential question. It affects many people. Most people in working-class neighborhoods end up being represented by public defenders who don't have the resources to move forward: merely getting a copy of the dossier requires time and money. One has to give both the defense and the victim the needed means to fully enjoy their rights as a citizen.

It must be possible for citizens to have free, easy, and full access to the judicial system. When you attend a trial, whether it is at Bobigny or elsewhere, you see people's poverty and distress: it's a beggar's alley. Even the judges have no resources. How do we explain this in a republic and in a democracy? If the judicial system is independent, then it must make it possible for people to be free and be allowed to act. But independence and freedom, for all that, aren't a license to be irresponsible. People don't have the means to truly defend themselves in front of the judges. The judicial system, the police—it's the same struggle. Everyone talks about the police in the *quartiers*, but do they know the conditions under which the police work? The offices are dilapidated; it's extremely rough. We have to give this public service the resources it needs to do its job correctly. In a few years, there will be more men and women from working-class neighborhoods on the police force. To be a guardian of the peace, in public service, you don't need to have a college education. Many children of the working classes will become cops, and we'll suddenly find a lot of blacks and Arabs on the police force. Will we continue to say then that our police force is racist? That argument won't hold. Today, every time the police intervene in one of our neighborhoods, they're treated as racists. I think it's necessary to watch that kind of talk. Sometimes it's true; the police are off base. But you have to have the courage

9. The *Cour de cassation* is France's court of last resort, although it is structured differently than the Supreme Courts in the United States and Great Britain. —Trans.

to look things in the face and not systematically assume that they are guilty of every misdeed. The police often do thankless work.

FADELA: The Outreau affair touched all of us. Any one of us could have been declared guilty and imprisoned on any given day. Lives were ruined for no reason, because of pathological lies. The judicial system was shown to be unjust. One thing is sure: the police and the judicial system operate by different rules. A police mentality makes young people feel unsafe, and the justice system provokes a sense of injustice. We have to fight against both of these.

Let's begin by fighting for decent conditions. I often accompany people to the police station to help them. The stations are a catastrophe; they're unsanitary. There are fifteen square meters for three offices; you can't even walk around in them. I was dismayed when the female police officer who received me yesterday in a police station in the 20th arrondissement told me not to move the chair I was sitting in so that I wouldn't obstruct her colleagues as they went to the other offices. I often have the impression that I'm in a police station from the seventies. The only thing that has changed is that now the police have computers, although even those are old. The lack of funding leaves the police feeling that their work isn't recognized.

Social Violence

FADELA: I am not in favor of repression. I don't believe in zero tolerance for delinquency, in the housing projects or anywhere else. Remember, there are rich kids who commit acts of delinquency, too—although if you have the means to pay a good lawyer, you come out in better shape. We have to strike a balance and look for a middle ground to find measures that prevent the slide into delinquency. But at the same time, kids do have to be punished, and pedagogical measures have to accompany this punishment. When judges talk to young delinquents, what they say isn't convincing and doesn't work. The kids don't understand. When they are punished, they couldn't care less, because they're not in the right frame of mind to understand; they're not aware. It's up to the police to explain to kids why they have been arrested. And once the kids are found guilty, they shouldn't be left without explanations, without guidance. We have called on the president of the Republic to establish educational alternatives in prisons, with pedagogical and citizen follow-up, so that kids do come to understand and don't start up again. We're well aware today that for many of them, prison becomes a sort of education in delinquency. No one is addressing this; there's no ongoing training. We must help them find a way out that will keep them from ending up back in prison, but we hit a wall when it comes to financial and human resources. Repression, that doesn't lead to anything.

MOHAMMED: The repressive dynamic has never been a solution to anything. I'll give you an example: the debate over military supervision of students in working-class neighborhoods, introduced by Ségolène Royal. If we're talking about second-chance schools, yes, but if it's a question of assigning them to military regiments to learn discipline, then no. Because the role of the army in the collective unconscious, the popular unconscious, is not to maintain order, but rather to wage war. What matters is living together, progress, the general interest, civic spirit; those are the notions that will mobilize citizens. The French public has a good grasp of the situation. They know the difficult reality: children are victims of violence in schools, whenever you take public transportation you're exposed to violence, some people can't find a job, and others are laid off. Basically, violence is no longer something abstract for the French. It's a daily reality. They oppose all these forms of violence, but they are capable of acts of solidarity. In my opinion, we need to raise civic awareness. If political institutions want to be in the game, they must attempt to restore normalcy to the situation. Neither angelic prevention nor repression, just a system that gives all citizens, whatever their social class, the opportunity to raise themselves up. Law is only the codified part of political discourse. It must teach respect for the rules. At the moment, there's an escalation in the political discourse and in the repressive measures; that won't lead anywhere.

FADELA: Oh, yes it will! This verbal escalation, this move toward ever more security, it isn't going to bring just a copy to power, it's going to bring the original! I'm convinced of it. One of two things has to happen: either we fight for the concept of living together and we give ourselves the means to do it, or we have the courage to say that it's no longer possible. In the latter case, we end up creating ghettos to enclose the excluded. They'll survive there, after all. People are already being concentrated in pockets of relegation where they accumulate social handicaps. The jolts of violence that occur in the housing projects are presented as a danger, and they are treated dramatically; hence the violence escalates. And yet they are only one example of violence, even though they are treated as the height of violence.

We live in an anxiety-prone society. Violence is everywhere: on TV, in advertisements, in video games, etcetera. For a woman, it's terrible to see the growing number of photographs of naked women on city streets selling everything and anything. It's a form of violence that permeates all our lives. We certainly won't be able to eradicate it or curb it by escalating things or employing a logic of total repression; that will lead only to the opposite result. I am convinced that we need to invest in education in order to eradicate violence. But that means spending money and desegregating populations. We need to promote social *mixité*; that's tremendously important for the concept of living together. We also need to encourage the restoration of parental authority and try not to guilt-trip parents or point fingers at them. Making social aid to families subject to official oversight is ridiculous. We have to understand that this aid is an integral component of family budgets. Without such assistance, some families would not be able to eat. We really have to invest in all aspects of education, both in family policy and in national education, including the management of urbanization policies.

MOHAMMED: We must never forget the social violence that's always hanging over us and that causes such devastation. We can't treat physical violence by ignoring social violence. I don't think we take proper account of the damage it does to people's minds. There are people who work twenty years at a company, and then they are chucked out with no explanation! You find this type of social violence—you feel it—in working-class neighborhoods. You can sense it in the attitudes of young people and in those who are asking themselves if tomorrow they will be able to make a living, or find a job, or begin working on a degree. It's a simple question that all French people ask themselves, whether or not they are immigrants, or black or white. Faced with the impossibility of a future, people create postures that can lead to things that are much more serious and nightmarish. This is exactly what is happening in working-class neighborhoods. Women's situation has reached a tipping point; sexism, violence, homophobia, and antisemitism have also increased in worrisome proportions. But no one seems to have noticed that all these ills arose in the same period. The deterioration of social conditions and a political void created a space that has become fertile ground for just about anything. Today we are discovering profound unrest.

If I took on this fight through Ni Putes Ni Soumises, it's because I became aware of this trend and the prevailing confusion. Of course, denouncing something isn't yet explaining it, but you have to have the courage to break taboos.

On France's Jewish television station, they were recently talking about the Ilan tragedy and the demonstration that followed.[1] Some friends who are of the Jewish faith, talented journalists and experienced commentators, told me with regret that when a youth of immigrant origins, Arab or Muslim, becomes the victim of such an act, nobody does anything. This made me remark that people often use two sets of weights, two different measures. I responded to them that this is a discourse that I find very dangerous. Behind the appearance of responsibility and generosity, this discourse is detrimental because it validates the logic of "us and them." My responsibility as a citizen is to say no and to be the first to say "This concerns me." I went to the demonstration after Ilan's murder. I didn't see it as a Jewish demonstration; I didn't see it as any one community's demonstration. I saw that a French citizen had been the victim of a barbarous act with overtones of antisemitism. I experienced it as something tragic. If I took part in this demonstration, it's because I felt responsible. We must be vigilant about the communitarian discourse that is increasingly permeating political discourse in this country.

When you examine this discourse closely, you get the impression that our elected officials now admit that French society is made up of juxtaposed

1. Ilan Halimi was a young Jewish Frenchman who was held by gang members and tortured for more than three weeks in February 2006 in a suburb just south of Paris. He died on the way to the hospital. His death drew national and international attention because of the openly antisemitic and pro-Muslim rhetoric of the gang members. Twenty-seven people (ten women and seventeen men) were charged in connection with Halimi's murder. Several members of the gang were juveniles. —Trans.

communities and not of free and equal citizens. Political discourse is then adapted to each circumstance and to each community. I suspect that some think that people of immigrant origins represent a new electoral mass with specific demands, some sort of political bloc. They found a common denominator for this political bloc and designated it the Muslim bloc. Nowadays people disagree over who speaks for Muslims. It doesn't matter what kind of situation Muslims find themselves in, or what their future will be, or what will happen to women, or to these youths; these people couldn't care less. The essential thing is to say that Muslims are oppressed so that they can get their hands on the bloc. That is my profound conviction. But there is no such bloc, no electoral capital to utilize. There are men and women who are suffering, who have the same dreams, the same desires, and the same difficulties as so many other people. Flattering them is just as irresponsible as discriminating against them. It would be much more appropriate to make an effort to help them get out of this confinement, out of this social and mental ghetto in which we put them, and in which they allow themselves to be confined. The fight that Ni Putes Ni Soumises is leading is a veritable godsend for French society, particularly for those who allow themselves to be imprisoned in the mentality of victimizing discourse. It's a vehicle of emancipation for everybody. Ni Putes Ni Soumises is contributing to the "democratization of good sense."

FADELA: On the topic of politics, I'm going to be frank and very honest. Safety is a right; it's the least that we can demand from a democracy and a state of law. If you look at the facts, neither the left nor the right has responded to this demand. No one has a monopoly on this issue, because everyone has a need to live calmly and tranquilly, in peace and harmony with others, whatever their ethnic origin or religion may be. In order to achieve this, we have to broach this issue with lucidity and agree on the concepts we use. Those of safety and insecurity [*sécurité et d'insécurité*] do not work in the same register. Safety can be measured, quantified, and evaluated. Insecurity has a psychological dimension that remains difficult to grasp. The spectacle of insecurity that we witness today seeks only to stimulate fear. Talking about insecurity leads us to associate terrifying images with the discourse. When we speak about insecurity today, we immediately think "immigrants, children of immigrants, or the poor working class." Suddenly we are brought back to the unrest of the *banlieues* during the 1980s, to the era of joyrides. Everyone should feel involved. We have to move away from these mental associations that necessarily conjure up an image of national fragmentation. Ni Putes Ni Soumises subscribes to a position meant to clear up the conditions that allow insecurity to flourish. We have to find the middle ground between too much repression and too much laxity. The middle ground exists, but our politicians on both the right and the left don't seem to have heard of it yet. The left won't take up this particular debate, and the right is too caught up in radical discourse. Finding the middle ground means finding a way to talk about the right to safety for everyone in every domain.

I think that Ni Putes Ni Soumises exists precisely because the right to safety is lacking, but there are also things lacking when it comes to housing, work, professional development, and school. In a democracy, this issue should not drive a wedge between the left and the right, because it's the minimum in a state of law. Crime [*insécurité*] continues to be a polemical subject: some immediately feel stigmatized when the topic comes up, and others feel wronged by the absence of a response. If we're going to pull ourselves out of this fruitless, and perhaps even dangerous, cycle, I think that a clear program needs to be proposed that will include all of our fellow citizens. To resolve this crisis in a way that makes everyone feel responsible, we need to organize Special Assemblies on this issue everywhere, particularly in the housing projects.

MOHAMMED: I think that French society is currently suffering from the lack of a clear, precise, and well-defined social program. That generates anxiety and feeds feelings of uncertainty. Where is the left that we imagined? Where is the left that represents democracy, freedom, and progress? I get the impression that it has gotten stuck in the comforts of power and gotten used to political oscillation. But France can't wait. We need to have the courage to pull ourselves out of this mindset. When you hear politicians speak, you see that they're just sitting there waiting for the opposing camp to fall flat on its face in order to seize power. I think that the vast majority of the French have had enough. I hope that during the presidential elections next spring, France will have the level of debate that it deserves, and that the French will be able to make an informed choice. France needs a completely new alternative discourse on the issues of France and the French, France and Europe, and France's relationship with Africa, the rest of the world, the environment, AIDS, and all the problems at stake today.

FADELA: From the perspective of someone like me, I think that we're in a difficult situation, perhaps not one of social war, but a situation of social struggles. I think that we must achieve a position of equality. Each person must become an agent in his or her own life, and at the same time be able to demand a better life; it's just that our institutions are not sufficiently representative. I think that our country's democracy is suffering. I don't like the concept of "participatory democracy," because in my opinion it lacks substance. There are too many people who abstain in each election, and that's a sign that doesn't lie. Blank ballots are not taken into consideration. We don't really know the number of people who are contesting politics. It's easy to see that there are real difficulties within unions, and even within nonprofit organizations. We are not sufficiently representative, even though I'm of the opinion that certain activist organizations continue to play an important role in contesting power and struggling against the established order, both in working-class neighborhoods and in different regional collectives, whatever their political leanings. I don't know that we can talk about social war, but one thing is certain: there is too wide a gap between the rich and the poor in our country.

MOHAMMED: We are experiencing the prelude to an inevitable social confrontation. It's not going to happen ten years from now; the writing is already on the wall, it's already here. I have proof of this: Fadela and I were on the ground during the riots in the *banlieue*. I was struck by the fact that the French were afraid. And this fear was real and palpable. When Fadela wanted to write a letter to the president of the Republic asking him to pardon minors found guilty of punishable misdemeanors, we approached several journalists and found no support among them. Many of them were against our position. Paradoxically, the support we did find came from police officers and magistrates. It was as if the fact that they were on the ground themselves, in the middle of this tragic face-off, made them experience this reality firsthand. The real issue isn't the fear itself, but understanding it! What happened in the *banlieue* was not unheard of. I still remember how violently farmers fought for their rights, when public buildings were burned. I remember the workers who, out of desperation, wanted to contaminate the water supply because their factories were closing. I am astonished by this irrational fear of the *banlieue*, as if it's populated by barbarians. In this violence and in the spontaneity of these unplanned confrontations, I see the prelude to a social confrontation. People don't fear prison or anything else; they've simply had it with injustice. Political elites and institutions should know that people's everyday life is such that, at this point, they no longer fear anything. The dignity of the citizen has been jeopardized, and so we should expect people to make demands. We must give them the chance to act and to claim their rights, but within the framework and with the means granted to them by the Republic. For me, the Republic is not complete. It is our responsibility to build it; it's a project for today and tomorrow. Those who criticize it under the pretext that its values—liberty, equality, and fraternity—haven't become a practical reality on the ground either are mistaken in their analysis or have a Machiavellian outlook. In reality, those values, which haven't been articulated everywhere, are both the means and the ends. As long as the ends haven't been achieved, we must take hold of the means in order to demand these ends.

This is why I agree with Fadela that participatory democracy often serves only to put people to sleep by making them think that they're going to decide. Instead, we should strengthen the power of our elected officials, whether it's on the local or the national level, while at the same time promoting and organizing a system of checks and balances among citizens, by increasing the scope of referendums, by promoting our right to petition. Collective expertise exists. Citizens must be given the capacity to be vigilant and constantly on the watch for injustice. We have to keep this energy up because we need it. We have to mobilize young people, citizens; we have to breathe a little life back into democracy. Democracy feeds on itself; if it stagnates, it dies. Today we suffer not from too much democracy, but from not enough. People have pragmatic intelligence. I notice it every day in my work as a grassroots activist. I love people for that.

FADELA: I have only one fear. During the urban rebellions, some people did not use the tools of democracy. Personally, I'm not afraid of them rebelling—I hope they will rebel against injustice—but I fear that they will not use the weapons of the Republic to demand their rights. Maybe by now nothing can satisfy their anger. We have to work fast, then, to find new methods. If we do not win on this front, multiple mini-rebellions will break out, ending in unprecedented violence and repression. And we still won't have understood. I would have liked to see some leaders come out of this rebellion. In terms of discontent, it isn't that different from what we were going through in the eighties. They bear the stigma of poverty, and they are making the same claims. Most of our fellow citizens are interpreting the lack of political response as a decline in democracy. Neither the left nor the right is proposing real changes for people's everyday lives. Extremist elements are taking advantage of that, and they are beginning to encroach on our ground, and to circulate discourses that could be dangerous for the Republic and for France.

The Future

FADELA: How can we look forward and not aspire to an egalitarian society, in which men and women have the same rights and live in serenity, in relationships of peace and mutual respect? This vision is the very essence of Ni Putes Ni Soumises' struggle. Of course, the only way we can get there is to take one step at a time. One of the first steps has been to try to create a general awareness of the terrible living conditions for women in the housing projects, but also throughout the world. We are part of an international struggle, and we are hammering away to build the movement at this level. Construction has begun; it's an enormous undertaking, and it's going to be a long process. We have the will to change people's attitudes, and we want to do it in a way that reaches young people: young people here, young people in Europe, and also young people abroad.

This is happening through awareness campaigns and campaigns focused on prevention, like the *Guide to Respect*, which is a terrific tool. But it can also happen when someone—a parent, a teacher, a program leader, or an instructor in a community center, for example—intervenes in the life of a child and takes up the same ideas. Everyone has to have the same consistent message when educating children for equality to take root. We have to mobilize our efforts synergistically to save these children. The role of national education is of primary importance, which is why we're going to increase the number of programs we conduct in schools in collaboration with teachers and administrators. These teams of professionals are essential in the fight against violence against women and for equal rights. I applaud them, because I know the obstacles they face and their readiness to go the extra mile.

At each stage, we have to be able to offer relevant perspectives, and ones that correspond to the struggle for equality in all of its dimensions. The movement's university has become an essential event for doing this.[1]

Every day has its own work to be done: building, consolidating, developing; these are the engines that will drive me in the coming years.

MOHAMMED: In my view, the struggle we have led has already produced two victories. First, Fadela has brought a new feminist struggle to light, an urgent feminism, which affects people's everyday life and personal experience. The code of silence has been broken, and from now on the public will know what is happening in certain neighborhoods. Even the 8th of March has regained its former luster.[2] Secondly, the work of Ni Putes Ni Soumises prevented a challenge to one of our most fundamental principles: *laïcité*. Participation in the debates organized by the Stasi Commission was enlightening. All the more so as many people, tired of what was happening, thought that it was imperative to reflect and rethink a modified *laïcité*. Fadela told them that they had it wrong. It's a question of a principle that must be preserved; the social body has to be strengthened. We need this booster shot.

In ten years, after all is said and done, we will be able to measure the work that has been accomplished and see the great service rendered to the Republic, a Republic that was beginning to doubt itself but which then took stock of the reality in working-class neighborhoods.

The sense of belonging to the nation, to the Republic, has to be revived. In spite of the difficulties, we do actually share values, and even if words are our only means, they allow us to change our everyday life. It is precisely these values that were used by women to gain the right to vote more than two centuries after the French Revolution. It is not a question of skin color, but of struggle within a democratic framework, because the Republic is still unfinished.

As for the rest, confrontation remains problematic because politics are difficult. Things are clogged; this country is governed by oligarchies. Sometimes I get the feeling that there's an understanding between these oligarchies, whatever their political or religious differences. It's time to break away from this way of operating, which has nothing to do with the tradition of the Republic. We need a clean break. I'm delighted that the word "republican" is currently in fashion: it's on Sarkozy's lips, and Ségolène's; Besancenot has

1. Since its inception, the movement has organized a weekend teach-in that it calls the Université Ni Putes Ni Soumises. The event draws hundreds of feminist activists to work together on the issues that matter most in their communities. —Trans.

2. March 8 is International Women's Day. Traditionally there is a march in Paris on this day. —Trans.

used the word, as have many others, because it is a necessity.[3] Citizens have to be given the chance to find the place they deserve. In this way, we will be able to create a world in which we can live together. I am equally delighted to see that the question of diversity is in fashion; everyone is talking about it. It was practically portrayed as an exceptional event that there should be a black newscaster! In the twenty-first century. This is something that should have been normal. But we have to continue in order to create the preconditions for the exercise of freedom. We are approaching the second phase. A new way for men and women to live together in equality, a new way to envision living together, a new way of building together with others.

FADELA: One thing is certain: Ni Putes Ni Soumises has had an effect on the debates, and notably on the debate over religious symbols. While some wanted to reduce the veil to its religious connotation, NPNS's struggle for the emancipation of women and for the equality of the sexes really helped to shake that assumption, in particular at the moment of the Stasi Commission. It became of primary importance for the feminist movement to finally look into the situation of women in working-class neighborhoods.

I believe that there is no more beautiful struggle in the world than the struggle for human rights. I believe that the best way to give meaning to one's own life is to become invested in the lives of others.

3. Olivier Besancenot was the Revolutionary Communist League candidate in the 2007 presidential election in France.

Part III

Reflecting on the Path

Resistance and Controversy

An Interview with Fadela Amara

In Racaille de la République, *you express the hope that people in housing projects and at-risk neighborhoods will continue to rise up against the injustices they suffer, but you also say that your greatest fear is that such revolts will be violent rather than working with the tools provided by republican democracy. You call for new methods of addressing social problems and suggest that without them the situation is likely to degenerate further, giving rise to increased street violence as well as to unprecedented levels of police repression. Can you talk about the origins of your commitment to nonviolent political action, and specifically about the new programs and methods you hope to develop as minister of urban policy to improve conditions for people living in the* banlieues *and to aid them in their fight for justice?*

So, the engagement with nonviolent activism goes back to when I was fourteen years old. It was due, certainly, to an extremely violent awakening, because I lost my brother to a car accident, a car driven by a drunk driver, and I found out that the police officers made racist comments to my mother. That was unacceptable to me. After that, I decided to take up the struggle against all forms of injustice, but in an extremely pacifist way—because I'm a great admirer of Martin Luther King and a great admirer of Gandhi. And I find that the men who fought not for themselves but for all of humanity, for all the civil rights of people like them, well, we saw what that accomplished. It marked their time, but it also marked the history of humanity. And as for

This interview was conducted by Brittany Murray and Diane Perpich in July 2007 at Fadela Amara's new offices as Secrétaire d'Etat chargée de la politique de la ville. We kindly acknowledge her permission to publish this interview. —Trans.

me, I was highly influenced by their struggles. And so as a result, when I became aware of things that weren't right, I decided, since they had opened the way, to take the same path. But modestly, obviously. On a smaller scale, using their methods to make a change.

Could you talk about the new projects and methods that you hope to develop as minister of urban policy to improve the situation for those living in the banlieues *and to support them in their struggles for justice?*

As far as my method of working is concerned, it's going to be a little bit unique, because all of the urban policy programs that have been established by different, successive administrations over the past twenty years—whether by a left- or a right-leaning government—these programs, and urban policy, have always been worked out in the abstract, and then were imposed as a whole set of initiatives to be implanted into the *quartiers*. Never has anyone consulted the populations living in these at-risk neighborhoods so that they can make these projects their own. So as for my working method now . . . Obviously there are things we are going to keep, things that work, that were put in place by preceding administrations, but we are going to enrich the urban policy program. We'll keep certain initiatives, building on them, making them more relevant, and evaluating them as well; but most of all, we're going to change the method.

By that I mean that there is going to be a major public consultation to permit the people who live in these precarious neighborhoods to appropriate urban policy for themselves, to become actors in urban policy. They will no longer be passive citizens who are going to be subjected to something. On the contrary, they will play a vital and central role. *They* are the ones who are going to become the actors of this urban policy. *They* are going to participate in developing policy, making proposals, thinking them over, and even evaluating the results. Specifically, that means that one year after we have put everything into place, we are going to evaluate the policies and initiatives we've carried out. It's the inhabitants of those neighborhoods who are going to tell us what worked and what didn't. They are going to tell us how they see things. We're going to practice community-informed politics [*une politique de proximité*], and I think that it's a revolutionary method, in fact. Nobody wants to do that, because first of all it requires a lot of courage. You have to go to the *quartiers*. For certain politicians, well, that's a little bit complicated. So this kind of politics requires courage, and then it requires most of all a desire to change political practices. You have to be ready to stir up a hornet's nest, as they say, and most of all, you have to breathe life back into politics and take it back to its roots. Because I can't conceive of politics except insofar as it is in the service of human beings. Otherwise there's no point.

In the late 1980s you signed a petition in support of allowing girls to wear headscarves in school. This was understood at the time as a cultural *rather than* religious *[*cultuel*] symbol, and the act of wearing the veil in school symbolized recognition of the equal rights and equal worth to be granted to Muslim students. The rise of Islamic communitarianism and its effects in France's housing projects and at-risk neighborhoods changed your views on this question. Contesting headscarves in the schools became a way of protecting Muslim women's rights to equal treatment and to the full benefits of French citizenship both in private and in public. We think that people will understand the change in your views, but they may still wonder if you don't go too far in your opposition to the veil and in your embrace of the values of the Republic. After all, aren't Muslim women still in need of recognition of the value of their individual choices and their religious and cultural identities* as *Muslim women? And haven't the republican values of equality and* laïcité, *because they've remained values in name only or have remained abstract and formal, fallen far short of the goal of giving all of France's citizens the same right to a secure and tranquil life?*

Well, it's a fairly complicated situation. It's true that in 1989, when the first girls showed up in school wearing the veil, right away I joined the camp of those who defended them. I was betting on the public school system, which for me has an essential mission: educating people to be citizens of this country. Everything happens through education. Knowledge is transmitted and citizens are brought up through a project of commitment to republican values: liberty, equality, fraternity. It just so happened that in precarious neighborhoods, which were—which *are*—in the process of social decomposition, the schools were falling apart in the same way at the same time. That means that to the extent that violence was showing up in the housing projects, it was also showing up in the schools—schools that I call ghetto schools. So, in fact, what started as two girls became a hundred girls, two hundred, then three hundred, and so on.

You have to understand that the mentality is different than it was in '89, when girls wore the veil as a cultural claim. It was about belonging to a certain identity category, even perhaps a civilization. Up against an extremely difficult context of racism, infringement, exclusion, etcetera, this identity was carried like a banner. It was an affirmation for recognition of a certain identity, and most of all, it was affirmed with a certain dignity. Then something unexpected happened. On top of the mass unemployment that affected the *quartiers,* on top of exclusion from a Republic that didn't want to recognize all its children—discrimination is extremely prevalent in this country, still today, and we have to fight it whatever the cost—there was also the creation and implantation of Islamist sects that took off at this particular time.

From then on, this communitarian system influenced by religious extremism pulled the rug out from under the French secular republican system. And so, in fact, we found ourselves in a situation where you had an entire segment of young people in the *quartiers* rushing into Islamism. Be careful to make the distinction between Islam as a religion, as a faith, and the political exploitation of Islam called "Islamism," which is not the same thing and which must be fought at all costs. It's what I personally call "green fascism," green for the color of Islam, Islam as a political program. From then on, during all those years, we saw a tremendous number of girls and boys, but especially girls, give up their rights.

That really needed to be stopped in its tracks. It needed to be pushed back. And to stop it in its tracks, it was precisely people like me, who are of the Muslim faith, believers—I'm not an atheist—who needed to participate in this battle for liberty, for fraternity. I believe that universal values, the question of feminism and of women's rights, these are really central questions today for every political project throughout the world. I think that when we talk about dictators, and when we talk about social programs that oppress the individual, those kinds of regimes oppress women first. And that's why I am very much in solidarity with and attached to women's struggles worldwide. I think that in our country, the issue of cultural relativism is the topic of an extremely heated debate precisely because it begs the question posed by women's rights. I find that cultural relativism contributes to the isolation of immigrant women and women of immigrant backgrounds, and that is not acceptable. I believe that when we tolerate, or accept, the traditions of others because they have a different culture, well, that can come from good intentions, but it actually leads to a disparity in rights. And so a situation suddenly arises where we are participating in the oppression of women. And I just can't accept that.

It's true that universal values are, in reality, abstract, but they are the means to an extraordinary end: the liberties of the individual, and especially of women. And I think that's a struggle we must carry on in France, but also one that must be waged worldwide. I have always thought that liberty and equality are universal values. They don't belong to France. They don't belong to the West. They belong to humanity. These values are the West's contribution, and they are a legacy left to all of humanity.

I believe that in some countries, in the Middle East and the East in general, and particularly in Arab countries and Muslim countries, these universal values need to be appropriated. That's what progressive forces in those countries are doing, forces often led by women, forces supported by women who themselves know what oppression is because they are subjected to it. I think that the issues of liberty and equality cannot be redefined in accordance with the color of a person's skin. So I stand very much in solidarity with every feminist struggle throughout the world at the moment when all that we stand for, all the rights that women have gained, are being dismantled.

Can you imagine a time when social conditions would be such that the veil could truly reflect an autonomous, personal choice, and such that women would have the right to wear it in all public spaces?

Well, as for that, it is conceivable only when the veil is serving as a tool of emancipation. That's what is going on in Iran. The obligation to wear the veil under threat of death is very clear. Women are obliged to wear the veil in order to have access to public space, to have a social existence, and to be recognized as such. But Iranian women continue to think, and I continue to think, that the veil is not a religious symbol but rather the very seal of women's humiliation. In this whole affair, there is a political program, and it is a program aimed at oppressing individuality, especially for women. Women are forced to wear the veil just to have access to public space, not even to mix with men, but merely to exist as social entities. They have to wear it to enjoy the use of public space, to go to work, and to study. All these activities help them figure out how to begin the process of emancipation. But I don't know of any Iranian woman in my circle who doesn't continue to hope and to look forward to the goal of being able to take off this veil, because they know it remains, all the same, a symbol of the submission and oppression of women. And that's very important. Anyway, the veil today—there's a real fight being led at this moment by Iranian women, among others. There is an entire liberation movement coming together, but there is also an unprecedented repression of this movement by the Iranian regime. That's why we have to be extremely watchful and stand in solidarity.

You've described NPNS as a bridge spanning the gap between feminism and the lives of the women in the housing projects. This is undoubtedly a difficult position to be in. Contemporary feminist struggles such as the fight for parity have seemed largely irrelevant to women in the banlieues, *where there are more fundamental needs and where feminism is certainly not fashionable in any case.*

At the same time, mainstream feminism is struggling with the perception that it is a movement whose time has come and gone in the struggles of the sixties and seventies. How successful has NPNS been as a bridge to feminism, and what remains to be done to bring these two groups of women together?

I believe that Ni Putes Ni Soumises succeeded in meeting an extraordinary challenge. First it was breaking the silence among women in the *quartiers* who belong to the working class and who weren't at all, I would say, led to, and had no direct relation with, the classical feminism of the seventies. I blame past feminisms for abandoning the women of the *quartiers*, who belong to the disadvantaged classes, and for closing their eyes to all the forms of oppression imposed by the patriarchal society and the communitarian mode of operation—influenced by religious extremism—that exists and persists in the housing projects. When Ni Putes Ni Soumises initiated a process of breaking the silence, we called public attention to something that was supposed to be impossible in this country, France, which supposedly represents the Rights of Man with a capital M. We made visible, for everyone to see, that the oppression of women exists in this country, a terrible oppression: the practice of archaic traditions, forced marriage, polygamy, mandatory wearing of the veil, and so on.

When we brought this debate out into the open, into the public eye, some feminists helped the NPNS movement right away. They immediately stood in solidarity with us, because they knew that it was crucial to join in this emancipatory process. But there were other feminists who did not understand, who did not want to understand—for their own reasons. As for me, I was very clear and I stand by it: I denounced this latter feminism for being middle-class feminism. The most recent demands by feminists were political demands for parity. Now, excuse me, but parity doesn't speak to us in the housing projects, because we're in a situation where survival is the issue. The issue is fundamental liberties: the right to dress how one wants, to put on makeup, the right to see a man, and even the right over one's own body, which is one of the first claims of the feminist movement in France. In the projects, we don't have this right insofar as we're not allowed to question the doctrine of virginity because it represents the honor of the family or the honor of the neighborhood. Today, girls are under permanent control precisely because of this honor. They are made to shoulder something that is too heavy for them. And so the right to one's own body doesn't even exist in the projects.

That's why I charged feminists with forgetting us. I basically told them, "You have actually betrayed the feminist cause because you have forgotten us. Yours is a middle-class feminism, in that your claim basically comes down to parity in a political system that itself remains extremely sexist. But all the same, don't forget half the population by merely saying, 'They'll manage on their own.'" So I was very harsh, very firm in my position. But at the same time, I think that parity has to be seen through, demanded, but without forgetting that there are women in our country who are oppressed simply because of their ethnic background.

All the progressive forces need to come together so that we can continue the feminist struggle collectively. There is one feminism, I would say, that claims freedom and equality for all women regardless of their skin color. And then there is this so-called feminism that is politically exploited by leftists—the far left—a feminism that is helping to establish a political program through extremely shameful alliances, alliances with Islamists. Some people assume that Islamism is a revolutionary program that will bring about a revolution in and of itself, one that could oppose or curb American imperialism. And under this pretext, people close their eyes to the oppression of women organized within this political program and through these particular alliances. That is scandalous, and we've denounced it; and unfortunately, that shocked certain feminists who were, themselves, for the veil.

In my opinion, if the issue of the veil is considered in absolute terms, it is conceivable that women, in the name of the right to choose and in order to protect individual liberties, might decide to say, "It's my choice. It's my right to wear the veil." We've heard this over the past few years. But in my assessment, in the *quartiers*, I can theoretically understand respecting this choice in the absolute, or in principle, but I can't accept it in practice. Why? Because not all of all the conditions for free choice regarding this decision have come together. There are all the forms of pressure and oppression that exist. So the girl, whether she wants to or not, doesn't actually get to decide for herself. She decides in light of her family structure, of the neighborhood, and the community's judgment. There are social, ethnic, and religious conditions. And so, in reality, she decides only through the prism of all these forms of oppression. And I think that in order to talk about the principle of individual liberty or the lack thereof, all the conditions that are going to permit her to freely decide have to be brought together. For the moment, in the housing projects, they have not come together.

Can you describe men's role in feminism and the NPNS movement?

I cannot conceive of the feminist struggle without men. I am absolutely not in favor of a battle between the sexes. All the same, I respect the fact that in the seventies, it was important for women to gather with other women because other spaces were extremely masculine, and women needed to be together to organize, etcetera. Of course, it was much more difficult then. But I sincerely think that it makes no sense today for the feminist struggle to be carried on only by women. That would mean losing half the battle and being no closer to winning the war. I think that the feminist struggle needs to be waged by women and for women, but also by and for men. So it's a struggle for both men and women. That's the reason why at NPNS, boys were alongside us from the beginning to fight against the oppression of women and to claim the right to equality simply as such, equal rights simply as such. I think that one of the successes of NPNS was in getting boys to participate. They are not passive spectators, they are actors in this struggle. They are making claims in the same way, on an equal footing with others, with the girls of the *quartiers*. The second thing that is really important is that we succeeded in getting the boys from the housing projects to participate, because it's a big part of the challenge to get people to admit that there are not just oppressors in the *quartiers*, there are also boys who are just as committed to feminist struggles. These boys agree that gender equality is a relevant and compelling question for any society they would want to live in. This has to be shown, too.

In your writings and your actions, you have insisted upon the importance of both individual responsibility and collective action. You don't shy away from denouncing the broader social conditions that contribute to the ghettoization of the banlieues *and the resulting oppression of women; however, you also resist a discourse of victimization that blames everything on social problems. You've written, "Racism doesn't excuse everything. That is why I loathe the discourse of victimization disguised as generosity. In reality, this discourse doesn't urge those who suffer racism to live together with others; rather, little by little it pushes them to the side to live in submission and abandonment." You've described this process as a kind of mental ghettoization and lamented that "young boys and girls have interiorized all the tools of oppression." What kinds of concrete things have you heard in your discussions with youth that make you worry that they've internalized this discourse of victimization? What can be done now to encourage young people in the* banlieues *to take a proactive stance without excusing the society-wide problems that contribute to their situation?*

I believe that the great difficulty today is to undo this discourse of victimization that's popular with certain adults in the *quartiers*, with young people, and among educators and teachers. Any time that young boys or girls act out, it's assumed that they should be excused because they are victims of their father's unemployment, they live in extremely difficult conditions, and so on. That doesn't help to make them into responsible citizens. Quite the contrary. It contributes to the creation of irresponsible citizens who might go on to commit terrible acts tomorrow. And society will continue to excuse them under the pretext that they are poor.

I am not in agreement with that way of thinking, primarily because I was a victim of it. For years I was looked at in this way. Today I think that it's a dangerous discourse. That's why, by the way, with respect to my new responsibilities, I always say that in order to institute urban policy initiatives, one first has to make the people who live in these neighborhoods actors of urban policy, especially the youth. So it's a question of building a reality, of helping to construct and develop active citizens in the place of passive ones. We have to undo this discourse of victimization and at the same time make it so that the fight against exclusion and the fight against poverty become *their* fight through collective action.

These fights must be undertaken through movements they can sign on to, including movements led by associations, unions, political movements, and political parties. They must reappropriate the space in which they live, becoming conscious of the fact that they belong to a social class, as well as to a given community. And because they're not okay with the injustice under which they live, they will have to organize collectively to fight this exclusion and reclaim equal rights. As a gesture of respect toward the work they have ahead of them, they must be helped to understand that they have duties, but that they also have rights; and one doesn't come without the other. And within this entire story, there's a notion that is very important—the notion of respect for the individual. This includes self-respect, but also respect for the other, however the other might identify him- or herself—in terms of religion, gender, sexual orientation, etcetera. That's why it's really important for this type of consciousness-raising to take place, even if it needs to happen in the form of intellectual violence. That's the whole difficulty.

I think certain political parties, notably the left in general, bear a great responsibility for what has become of youth in at-risk neighborhoods. By excusing them, by infantilizing them, by constructing a paternalistic discourse of victimization, we wind up in a situation where even when they're adults, they are immature with respect to the notion of citizenship. And that is not acceptable. So I think today we need to be very clear. They are individuals; they are citizens of this country. They have duties. They have rights. And most of all, they have this very important notion, the notion of respect.

So together we must fight all the forms of injustice that they might experience, including discrimination, racism, and sexism. But they must also learn, through collective struggle, to reclaim their rights.

Can you explain in more detail exactly what this discourse of victimization is? What history or historical processes does it touch upon?

Well, it's something that started a long time ago, in my opinion, something specifically linked to the history of France. To give a brief overview, I think that in what we call the *quartiers*, that is, in what are working-class neighborhoods, the vast majority of the inhabitants are people who are immigrants or descendants of immigrants. Many of them came from places that were once colonies, and a certain discourse that was part of how populations were managed in the colonies continues to exist in France today. Now, to tell this history in a way that's less bleak, it has to be said that the *quartiers* are not exactly run like colonies, because, after all, these young people can vote when they're eighteen years old like everyone else. So there is an inequality, but it's not exactly the same as it was for their parents, who were truly the "indigenous of the Republic" when France occupied Algeria and held Morocco as a protectorate. In those cases, there weren't any of these civil rights.

In France, it's not the same now, but the paternalistic discourse remains. It's the way they still think about this kind of population because it comes from the old colonies; they have adapted the discourse they had at the time to today's youth, and so all of a sudden, these youth are allowed to do anything and everything. Because when they act out, when they mess up, people say, "Well, after all, it's not their fault. They are oppressed. They are excluded." This sentiment actually destroys the notion of respect for citizenship: it's because France was a colonizer and because these populations came from these colonies. Many of the people who work on issues related to the *quartiers* or who work within these neighborhoods bear a sense of guilt. This includes the left in general. Some leftists are really paternalistic toward this type of population because they feel guilty. The left doesn't want to recognize the fact that these people are also full citizens with rights and duties, citizens who must be treated as equal to any other citizen of this country.

Can you describe your role in organizing the Special Assembly of Women of the Quartiers *in 2002? Who were the women who were present, and what came out of this Special Assembly?*

I was the initiator of the Special Assembly, since it was organized by the Fédération des maisons des potes, which is an organization that brings together several associations that are present in the *quartiers*, and I was the president at the time. And as far as the women who were present are concerned, they were all from working-class neighborhoods, and that allowed us to discuss four themes during this Special Assembly: first, employment and education; then there was a committee on violence, another committee on sexuality, and a fourth committee, which interested me a little less, on traditions and religions and whether they are an obstacle to women's emancipation. And from these four working committees, we released a manifesto listing the demands of the women of the *quartiers*, which in fact distilled different propositions relating to all the themes—urban policy, family policy, and so on.

The second thing that came out of this Special Assembly is the famous petition "L'appel des femmes des quartiers," which became a national petition called "Ni Putes Ni Soumises." In this petition, there is a very clear, very strong text reclaiming liberty and equality. It received more than eighty thousand counted signatures. I refer to the number of counted signatures because there were still four big boxes, but we were overwhelmed. We could no longer tally all the signatures, the response was so enormous.

And where does the name "Ni Putes Ni Soumises" come from?

So, NPNS as a slogan! At the time, it was my doing. We were a team; we were discussing what we were going to do. And in fact, some were for a more neutral slogan, a less harsh one, and I said no. I said that it needed to reflect the reality of the situation, the deterioration of women's condition in working-class neighborhoods. And I said that since many youth in the *quartiers* say, "They're all whores, except my mother," it would be Neither Whores Nor Submissive. The "nor submissive" part is a response to the leftist intellectuals who "explained" on news talk shows that "if girls and women from the *quartiers* are in a situation of submission, it's because they don't protest." I was appalled by that statement, because many of those women participate in organizations that foster social cohesion. And through these organizations, they also demand a place, a status, respect. I found these leftist intellectuals to be a little bit arrogant and a little bit pedantic. So that's why. It's a way to respond to them, but it's also a way for me to pay homage to all these women from the *quartiers* who are getting involved.

The march must have been a political education for all of you who went, especially, perhaps, for the men and women of the group who were rather young at the time. Can you say a little bit about the ambience among the marchers during those five weeks together?

The march wasn't really set up as a political education, but as a key step toward breaking the silence, because the most terrible thing in working-class neighborhoods is the code of silence, the *omerta*. To explode the code of silence, we had to create an initiative that would kick things into gear, and that would promote open discussion. The young people who accompanied me on the march—boys and girls, because it was a mixed movement from the beginning—were not in the habit of speaking out in public. It's difficult to do, and they weren't used to it themselves. They had to break their own silence, while at the same time breaking the silence of the public who had come to see us. So it was sort of complicated. Of those who accompanied me, there were about two more besides me who had political training, since before setting out, I had already been an activist in the Socialist Party. There was another young girl named Loubna Méliane who was also an activist in the Socialist Party, but after the march she went back to SOS Racisme. She continued her activism. As for me, we created the official NPNS movement as soon as the march ended, and we continued to train the marchers who were with us.

But in fact, the idea at the beginning was not to train people in politics. Training people politically came as a second step. The first step was to encourage people to break the silence.

Were there ever moments during the march when you felt that you were in danger?

In fact, yes. Not so much during the March of Women against the Ghetto and for Equality. There we were more concerned with opening the way for a certain discussion, that is to say, explaining all the forms of violence that women in the *quartiers* experience, even those of a social nature; there is a lot of exclusion, unemployment, and poverty. This is especially true for women. Many women raise their children alone; they work, but under terrible conditions. So this was the discussion we wanted to open up. It was also about the physical and mental violence—the harassment—that the girls and women of the *quartiers* experience. Then there was also the task of denouncing all these archaic traditions that are making a strong comeback. This is especially an issue with respect to virginity; it is becoming a symbol of the family's and the neighborhood's honor. This conception of virginity is shutting women up in their own bodies, and more importantly, it is dispossessing them of their bodies because now they belong to the entire neighborhood. Their bodies belong to an entire group of men who can take the liberty of intervening when they think that the women are in a situation that could jeopardize their honor. So this was what needed to be said. We were not actually in danger, even if it was a little bit difficult because there were boys who didn't like what we were doing from the start. We weren't really in danger at that time.

It was in 2004 that we were really in danger, during the debate over *laïcité*. I used this frightening phrase: I said that we had to fight the green fascism of Islamism at all costs, meaning the political exploitation of Islam. Then I received my first death threat. That was the first physical threat; it came from that incident. But over the issue of denouncing violence against women in the *quartiers*: no. We had a few small problems, but nothing major. The first threat came for condemning "green fascism."

After the march, when you came back to Paris on March 8, 2003, how did it happen that NPNS was placed at the head of the march for International Women's Day?

First of all, I believe that at each of the twenty-two stages of the March of Women against the Ghetto and for Equality, the march became a little bit more powerful. That is to say, at the first stage there were no more than fifteen people. At the second, there were only sixteen. And then, afterward, something extraordinary happened. The media began to talk about this phenomenon. They were talking about this group of young people—boys and girls from the *quartiers*—who were traveling to twenty-two cities to break the silence surrounding the women of the *quartiers* and to denounce the deterioration of conditions for girls and women in the *quartiers*. It was the local newspapers, the local press, that actually publicized the march and got people talking about it. There was also an article in *Libération*, a national newspaper, that got the word out. After that, the Ni Putes Ni Soumises petition that we released in the *Nouvel Observateur* got people talking about the march.

In fact, we hadn't really counted on the media attention. The local papers called attention to this march, and suddenly we no longer found ourselves among fifteen or seventeen people. We were one hundred, two hundred, three hundred in number. In Marseille we were fifteen hundred. This was huge, huge, huge. And in fact, we were gathering force. When we arrived in Paris, the Collectif national des droits des femmes, which has been bringing together the feminist organizations of this country for a while now, was totally blown away by the extraordinary process unleashed by the march.

We had planned on organizing our own demonstration when we got to Paris to drive our point home nationally and symbolically. Demonstrating in Paris is extraordinarily symbolic. It was also meant to remind people of the March of the Beurs. Back then it was only the guys who took the floor, but this time it was women who were speaking. So it was also meant to reflect that, but it was much more open, because ours was not just a Beur movement; it was much bigger. It was women from the *quartiers*, no matter what their ethnic origins, and we denounced living conditions as well.

Demonstrating in Paris was important for us because we could see the success of our march. It was an extraordinary thing, one of the most rewarding things for us. The famous Collectif national des droits des femmes came along with us, and everyone demonstrated behind the slogan "Ni Putes Ni Soumises." That was the greatest victory, the first political victory.

You have fought to change conditions in the banlieues, *but you have also taken controversial positions such as your support of the law against wearing religious symbols in school. How would you respond to critics who argue that your opinions lend themselves too easily to interpretations that would maintain the status quo or justify racist, xenophobic, or classist attitudes? How have you avoided the appropriation of your discourse by the political right? And now that you are part of the government, how will you maintain your independence?*

So, first of all, on the denunciation of violence against women in the *quartiers*. In fact, this is a discourse that is on the brink, I would say. If it is manipulated for political ends, it can contribute to the establishment of repressive policies. Now, we could have chosen to be silent and say: "Fine, we'll let it go because we're afraid to say things, because the right, or the extreme right, might take advantage of it." Our other choice, since the left has been absent from this particular struggle, was to say, quite simply, "Enough." I decided to say "Enough." I said it as a woman of the left, precisely because I am committed to the issue of freedom and equality for everyone, including women who come from a modest background. I'm strongly committed to the idea that all the forms of violence that exist in the *quartiers* must be addressed in the same way as the types of violence that exist elsewhere. And so from that moment on, being insulted by the left didn't bother me. When they criticize or disparage Fadela, it doesn't bother me. What bothers me is closing my eyes, being complicit in the violence that exists in the *quartiers*. It bothers me not to denounce it as an activist working for the Rights of Man with a capital M.

I made that decision, and I stand by it. I think that all the pedagogical work, and my personal and family history, prevent a certain appropriation by the right. I have presented myself since the beginning as a woman of the left, with the values of the left. It is as such that I have denounced a certain left that is today allied with Islamists, among others, and in any case is complicit in the sense that it upholds the oppression of women in the *quartiers*. The left has closed its eyes to this oppression. Quite simply, this story of a woman who is an activist for the Rights of Man with a capital M means that the right cannot, at any particular moment, exploit this struggle for its own purposes. The right did it to some degree when it wanted to launch the struggle against forced marriage, but it did it with my permission. The right also did it a bit when it wanted to exclude the young girls who wore the veil to school, but it did it with my complete permission. Not only with my permission; I was an actor in this struggle, because I believe that the veil is more than a religious symbol for some. For me, the veil is the oppression and humiliation of women. It is part of a political program that advocates the separation of the sexes, and therefore advocates gender inequality. And I don't agree with this program. I have always fought it in solidarity with the women of the Maghreb who struggle against the veil because they know what it means; they live it every day, and they've paid dearly for it. So, too, with Iranian women today, who have taken the lead, and who suffer terrible repression because of their gender. So, basically, those who repress them generally know that if they lose out on the veil question, they will lose their political program. Maintaining control over women means maintaining control over a totalitarian political program. If they lose on this particular issue, they lose everything.

I didn't have qualms about denouncing things. On the contrary, I was very angry with those on the left who refused to do so, since for me the left has always represented the movement for liberation and social progress. The left was completely absent from that particular debate. So I hope that the left will ask itself some questions. It's not surprising, by the way, that the left in France systematically loses elections, because it has lost its direction, in the sense that it has lost its leftist values. So I think it will continue to lose elections if it doesn't evaluate its defeat, and if it isn't capable of truly reflecting on what it means to be a leftist today.

I don't have qualms about working with the right. Right now I am a member of the government, and I stand by it fully, at least in the area that especially concerns me, the question of urban policy. I believe that as a woman of the left, I don't have time to wait for the left to reconstruct itself in order to change things in the *quartiers*. If you recall, it was in power for a long time. And quite honestly, it did nothing but initiate a smattering of policies in the most endangered neighborhoods, policies that unfortunately led us to suffer more and more oppression. The left didn't really work to get at the heart of things to fundamentally change the situation for the people who live there.

Quite frankly, I don't have time to wait for the left to return to power, especially given the state it's in. In the *quartiers*, there's a sense of urgency for the people who live in these neighborhoods. If I have to enter into a rightist government to carry on this struggle so that things get better in the *quartiers*—particularly in terms of buildings and the environment, but also in terms of improving people's living conditions in general—then, yes, I'll go. It doesn't bother me, even if it upsets some of my friends. It must be said, all the same, that the vast majority of people I know on the left support my entry into the government. It's a personal story, too, a journey. I come from civil society: I am not a card-carrying member of a party. I left the Socialist Party a long time ago. So it's a personal story. Everyone, no matter what their political leanings, understood that there is a sense of urgency. It's worth remembering that the urban riots of November 2005 happened a year and a half ago. They understood very well that it is extremely urgent that we do something to change the situation in the *quartiers*.

What are the differences, either past or future, between being a voice of opposition from outside the government and being a voice from inside the government?

First of all, being outside is a much easier position, because it's a position where you systematically denounce things that the government does. Not everything. My strategy has always been to denounce the things that don't work, and on the other hand, to salute those that do. I don't want to oppose things just to oppose things. I don't have a political career to manage. So when I was the president of NPNS, my mindset was to denounce things that didn't work, but to salute the things that were promising, particularly for the people in the *quartiers*—or in any case, the things that we judged to be promising. This is, or *was*, more comfortable for me. The easy way for me would have been to stay at NPNS. But I think that at a given moment, after a certain amount of time, it is irresponsible to continue doing the same thing.

That's why I chose to join the government to change the situation for people in the *quartiers* from the inside. I believe that there is a time when you have to pass from criticism to construction to action. And in order to act, there is no better place to be than at the center of power. And to be at the center of power, you have to cross the threshold. You have to go there. So at least I know that the decisions I make today are working in favor of the people in the *quartiers*. I'm directly responsible. And insofar as I now belong to a government whose ideas I don't always share, my ability to intervene allows me to raise awareness about initiatives that might be instituted, things that I think could be harmful to people in the *quartiers*. Hearing this point of view in a rightist government also allows them to hear a different perspective. In any case, I am not alone. Martin Hirsch and others are with me.[1] Other people from the left make their voices heard as well, speaking out on specific topics.

I'll give you an example. On the issue of immigration, I had a tête-à-tête with Hortefeux.[2] We had an exchange about the law, about immigration, etcetera. He understood the difficulty we have in seeing the concepts of immigration and national identity jammed together, side by side. So then later we broadened the discussion to include integration policy, the policy of cooperation, and so on. For myself, and I wrote about this in *La racaille de la République*, I can't conceive of managing the flow of migration if we're not capable—at the national level in France and from a European perspective—of aiding economic development in those countries that migratory populations are coming from. These are countries that the population is leaving because they're having trouble surviving there. I believe that our responsibility in France, and particularly in Europe, is to help these countries develop themselves from an economic perspective so that people stay there. On the other hand, I'll say it again, even if it sometimes makes certain people shudder: I am very happy to welcome mass immigration in the case of tourism. If it is to encourage people to visit my country, there's no problem. I think that it would be irresponsible to make people believe that we're going to manage or stop immigration, to build barriers around France and Europe by putting up barbed wire everywhere when elsewhere people are dying. It can't be done, and it's irresponsible to make people believe that. There will never be zero immigration. It's not true. There will never be zero delinquency. There will never be zero immigration. So we need to be able to think this through intelligently. Thinking it through intelligently means protecting our own interests while protecting the interests of other countries as well. We are in a global village. That can be said from within government, in discussions among ministers. We can say it and others can hear it. That is also part of, or one of, the actions that can be led from within.

Have you encountered obstacles working with Christine Boutin, who has opinions in direct opposition to yours, for example on abortion or on laïcité*?*

Listen, she has a story. She's a woman with convictions. She has a different story from mine. I also have convictions. I have a particular story. We don't

1. Martin Hirsch is the high commissioner for youth and active solidarity against poverty in the current government. —Trans.

2. Brice Hortefeux is the minister of the interior in the current French government. —Trans.

agree on the question of abortion, and on others questions as well—civil unions (PACS), gay marriage, gay couples adopting children. I'm in favor, she isn't. That's it.

For the moment, our responsibilities—she works largely with housing, and I work on urban policy—don't lead us into debates about those other issues. Ours is sort of an atypical partnership. I accepted [my position] for the simple, good reason that I think there are urgent issues in the *quartiers*. So I'm supposed to be capable of moving beyond my prejudices about people. Besides, Ms. Boutin is much more of a humanist than people think, even if she is firm in her convictions. I don't share them at all. But I am also a woman with convictions. I don't count on convincing her to change her opinions. For the moment, we have a calm thing going, and that will work. If that begins to waver, however, I don't expect to cede any ground to her.

How do you imagine the future of the NPNS movement now that you have joined the government?

I believe, first of all, that the movement built itself up with a national team and local teams. The movement isn't Fadela Amara, fortunately! The proof is that it still exists even though I've left. All the better. On the other hand, I think it is absolutely crucial that the movement—and this is what I said when I was able to intervene at the NPNS's National Assembly meeting—remain a completely independent movement that goes beyond political divisions, just as it did when I led it and when I created it. That is to say that even if I have my political affinities, it was imperative that this movement negotiate political landscapes completely independently. Above all, it must not turn out to be the source of transmission for the views of a political party, whether on the right or the left.

Along with Mohammed, the secretary-general of NPNS, I succeeded at something: we really brought this movement to life above and beyond party politics. It must continue like that. That's very, very important. The new president, Sihem Habchi, must be able to say at certain moments: "That won't work, that will." She must be capable of this political discernment. She must be ready to pay tribute to what works and to denounce what doesn't work, whether or not Fadela is in the government. On that point we must be very clear. But above all, it is imperative that this movement focus on the question of women—on the question of women's struggle in France, but also in Europe, and from an international point of view. The movement received recognition from the United Nations. It must continue in this approach. It must not let go of the fight against all forms of obscurantism, no matter which religion, or which political instrumentalization of religion, is behind it. That's a major stake today.

NPNS must continue to work along these lines, to exist and perdure. It must have an international point of view, but not cede ground, and I mean the ground of the housing projects. NPNS must continue to exist in the *quartiers*. Sihem has to continue to be a woman from the neighborhood. She has to continue to go into the *quartiers*, she has to maintain contact with the women and the girls in the projects. That's extremely important, because that's the very identity of the NPNS movement.

Index

Brittany Murray is a PhD student in the department of French and Italian at Northwestern University. She worked alongside Ni Putes Ni Soumises (NPNS) activists while on a Fulbright Fellowship and attended the 2007 World Social Forum in Kenya as an NPSS representative.

Diane Perpich is an associate professor of philosophy at Clemson University, the director of the program in women's studies, and the author of *The Ethics of Emmanuel Levinas.*

The University of Illinois Press
is a founding member of the
Association of American University Presses.

Composed in 10.5/13 Adobe Minion Pro
with Whitney display
by Celia Shapland
at the University of Illinois Press
Manufactured by Sheridan Books, Inc.

University of Illinois Press
1325 South Oak Street
Champaign, IL 61820-6903
www.press.uillinois.edu